# Strangers in Their Own Land

## A HISTORY OF MEXICAN-AMERICANS

by Albert Prago

FOUR WINDS PRESS/NEW YORK

*By the same author*

The Revolutions in Spanish America

PHOTO CREDITS

BUREAU OF INDIAN AFFAIRS, DEPARTMENT OF THE INTERIOR, p. 61.

MEXICAN GOVERNMENT TOURIST DEPARTMENT, p. 20.

THE NEW YORK HISTORICAL SOCIETY, p. 98.

NEW YORK PUBLIC LIBRARY PICTURE COLLECTION, pp. 6, 10-11, 14-15, 17, 22-23, 28-29, 34, 40-41, 56, 98 (insert), 101, 103, 110, 136, 138-139, 154-155.

ORGANIZATION OF AMERICAN STATES, pp. 66, 71, 128-129, 148, 150.

UNITED PRESS INTERNATIONAL PHOTOS, pp. 141, 152, 162, 172, 177, 187.

WIDE WORLD PHOTOS, pp. 3, 159, 169, 180-181, 184, 192, 199, 203.

Published by FOUR WINDS PRESS
A Division of Scholastic Magazines, Inc., New York, N.Y.
Copyright © 1973 by Albert Prago
All rights reserved
Printed in the United States of America
Library of Congress Catalogue Card Number: 72-87077

To the countless,
nameless heroes of
all races and creeds
who fought for human
dignity. And to the
new heroes arising
from the young.

# CONTENTS

# STRANGERS IN
# THEIR OWN LAND

# CHAPTER I

# Introduction

"ONE KILLED IN LOS ANGELES RIOT AFTER A MEXICAN-American Rally" reads a headline in *The New York Times* of February 1, 1971. Television newscasts portrayed men, women, and children carrying signs emblazoned *"Viva la Causa!"*

Hardly a day passes without some event in Texas, New Mexico, Arizona, Colorado, or California involving *La Causa*—The Cause—of Mexican-Americans. There are protests, demonstrations, marches, meetings, debates, and discussions, all of which concern the many problems that plague America's second largest ethnic minority.

About 10,000,000 "Spanish-Americans"—persons whose origins lie in Spanish-speaking countries—live in the United States. Of the ten million, approximately fifty-five per cent are of Mexican origin or descent, most of whom live in the Southwest.

Periodically the plight of the Mexican-Americans gains the limelight, most recently as a result of César Chávez' brilliant and courageous leadership of the agricultural workers in California. For many decades the farm workers, particularly the long-suffering migrant workers, have struggled for survival. César Chávez provided the dynamic spirit in organizing "the unorganizable" and, after a strike that lasted five years, finally compelled the big grape growers and other large farm owners to recognize the farm workers' union and to accede to some of its most burning demands. The grape pickers strike became known as *La Huelga—The Strike. La Huelga* was national news for five years. In a particularly dramatic fashion, it spotlighted the generally deplorable conditions of the Chicanos (as many Mexican-Americans call themselves) throughout the Southwest. *La Huelga* was only one response to the many grievances of this minority. Together the multiple problems and grievances are popularly called *La Causa.* While it means different things to different individuals and groups, the term embraces the totality of the reaction of a resentful minority to the oppression that has lasted more than one hundred years. This neglected minority is awakening and calling the attention of the nation to its existence and to its problems.

Although there is no one leader of this stirring movement, and although there is no clear-cut national program, all the spokesmen of *La Causa,* in different ways, have common aims—to achieve equality and freedom.

"Who am I?"

Most people get around to asking themselves this question at one time or another. Obviously it does not deal only with simple identification: name and address.

Even that simple identification has within it some historical sense. You identify with your neighborhood and its history, with your parents and their history. Rather early in life, encounters with friends and authorities, such as those

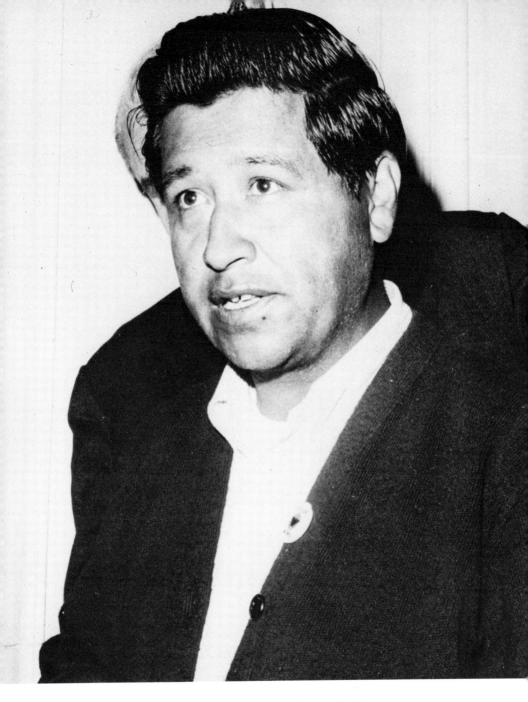

César Chávez, the dynamic leader of the
farm workers.

in school, often lead to questions about your past, like: "Were you born here?" "Were your parents born here?" And you may ask yourself whether you are first- or second- or third-generation American. And, precisely what significance does it have, what does it matter?

You learn that your past extends beyond that of your immediate neighborhood and beyond that of your immediate family. You are an American, and as such you are informed that you have a heritage. Great names and great deeds of the past are interpreted as part of *your* past. As an American, you may identify with a particular general, a hero, a President, or perhaps an inventor—all of whom are also Americans. A famous saying, a famous declaration, a famous speech, a great event—all aspects of American history become part of *your* history.

The heritage of the past is stretched further back, to foreign names connected with events preceding the founding of your country. Columbus discovered America. Cabot explored the northern coast. De Soto explored the Mississippi River. Another slice of the past is yours.

And the relevant past is stretched in other directions. Who were the Englishmen who first settled in this country? What was the England like from which they came? What ideas and institutions did they bring over? Is it not true that much of what is American was originally English? So, many English (and French, Dutch, and other European) traditions, ideas, and institutions become yours.

It is not long before you learn that English history has its past, and that other peoples and times are part of the continuous history of mankind. So, for example, you learn that the ancient Athenians contributed the idea of democracy (as well as the word itself), that the ancient Chinese invented the compass, that the ancient Jews contributed the idea of one universal God, and so on and on. Many streams of thought and many deeds converge over considerable time and countless places to mold your complex heritage and that of every other American.

Most Americans are hybrid, or hyphenated Americans. Irish-American, Italian-American, Russian-American; there are dozens of such dual nationalisms. Americans, therefore, claim a double heritage. One looks back with pride to one's American heritage and one also takes pride in the heritage stemming from non-American ancestors, whether immediate or distant. All Americans celebrate the Fourth of July; those of Irish extraction also celebrate St. Patrick's Day; of Italian, Columbus Day. At such celebrations, other Americans look on approvingly and very often the authorities give their official or semi-official endorsement.

Many of the hyphenated Americans, for example the Italian-Americans, had extreme difficulties in becoming assimilated. Complete assimilation seldom took place. Instead of the so-called melting pot in which, allegedly, immigrants and their descendants eventually lost all trace of their origins, it was more usual that they adopted American ways and at the same time retained many of the old customs.

Mexican-Americans had, and still have, problems similar to those that afflicted most immigrants. However the Mexican-American presents a special case. The Southwest was part of Mexico for more than three hundred years before its conquest by Anglo-Americans in the nineteenth century. The Mexicans who lived there were not immigrants to the United States. And while it is true that most Mexican-Americans today are the descendants of Mexican immigrants who crossed the border in the decades since 1848, many consider themselves native Americans whose heritage stretches back to a time long before the English, Dutch, or French settlements in the New World.

Mexican-Americans have, as do other groups, a mixed

An 1890 caricature of a "typical" Mexican
vendor in Texas by the western artist,
Frederic Remington.  Such demeaning portrayals
undoubtedly contributed to the existing
Texan—Mexican-American discord.

heritage, but this minority has been denied the fullness of
its heritage as have the American Blacks and the American
Indians. Some very important contributing streams of the
history of the United States, the contributions of Mexican-
Americans, have been neglected or distorted. For example,
histories of the United States abound with stories of the
heroism of the early pioneers who moved westward beyond
the Mississippi. Credit is given to them for the "opening of
the West." Yet many of those same histories give short shrift
to the exploits of Spanish and Mexican pioneers who explored and settled a major part of the trans-Mississippi
region long before the Anglo-American penetration.

Along with the errors of omission and distortion goes
second-class citizenship. The Mexican-American is considered inferior and his customs mocked or, at best, tolerated

in a patronizing way. People fall into the gross error of generalizing, and when one generalizes about people it leads to stereotyping. You may imagine a "frito bandito" as popularized in a television commercial; or a squatting, serape-draped, sombrero-hatted sleeping peasant, as depicted in the caricaturish statuettes bought by tourists. What is a "typical" Mexican-American? That is as absurd a question as "What is a typical American?" The skin color of Mexican-Americans varies from dark brown to white. Hair: black, brown, blonde. Tall, short; poor, rich. Occupation: from unskilled to professional. Religion: mostly Catholic; some Protestant, a few Jews. Diversity is the norm. Stereotyping, usually derogatory, hampers understanding people, and obstructs intelligent solutions to difficult problems.

Mexican-American. The hyphen is misleading for the heritage is multiple. The heritage is not only Mexican and American, but also Spanish; and for many it is also Indian; and for some it is also Black. A complex mixture? Yes, but each of us is the product of complex mixtures. All people have a mixed heritage, the precise nature of which varies in time and place and with each individual.

As is so often true for many peoples, the mixed heritage of Chicanos includes ancestors who often were one another's enemies. The Spaniard versus the Mexican; both against the Indian and against the Black. The Chicano who emphasizes one against the other does not resolve the perplexing difficulty. For example, the Chicano who exults in his Indian ancestry is ignoring the fact that he speaks Spanish, that his religion is, most likely, Catholic, and that some of his customs—like the kinds of food he eats—are often Mexican.

Because a major part of the mixed heritage of Mexican-Americans is Spanish and Indian, this history begins with the confrontation between the Spanish invaders from the old World and the Indians of Mexico in the New World.

> "...to serve God and His Maj-
> esty, to give light to those
> who were in darkness, and to
> grow rich, as all men desire
> to do."
> Bernal Díaz del Castillo

## CHAPTER II

# The Conquest
# and Its Aftermath

THE OCEANS OF THE WORLD ARE NOT OWNED BY INDIVIDU-
als nor by governments; they can be used by all. Some land, such as those put aside for city, state and national parks, is public; it also is open to be used by all. However, most of the land is owned by farmers, industrialists, banks, realtors, speculators, universities, churches and other individuals and institutions. Anyone who wishes to use privately owned land must pay someone for the privilege. This is a principal foundation of most modern societies, but it has not always been so.

When the first Europeans reached the New World, the local inhabitants—the Indians—used the land. The Indians plucked the fruits of the trees, caught the fish of the streams, hunted animals, cultivated the soil for harvests of maize (Indian corn) and beans and other staple edibles, extracted minerals to make tools and jewelry, used timber and mud and hides and reeds for housing, for furniture, for canoes. In a phrase—they all used the land. No Indian owned land. No Indian could buy or sell land.

For many decades after Columbus' great discovery, Spaniards came to the New World for "God, Gold and Glory." This compact phrase describes succinctly the religious motives of the missionaries who hoped to convert millions of Indians, and those of the rest of the Spaniards who hoped to achieve wealth, or power, or both. One way for obtaining gold and glory was to acquire land. The use of force in obtaining this land is the essence of the conquest of the New World.

How did the land in the New World come to be the property of the Spaniards? To answer simply "by conquest" conceals much. The specifics arouse indignation and consternation.

To the islands in the Caribbean on which he first set foot, Columbus gave new names, and claimed them in the name of the monarchs of Spain. Columbus thought that these islands were near Japan; by his own reckoning, however false, they were the property of the Great Khan. By what right, then, were they claimed for Spain? They were "discovered" by an Italian who had not even previously known of their existence. And Columbus' claim certainly was meaningless to the inhabitants of these islands.

Whether the natives were friendly or not, the claim was made quite meaningful by force of arms. The land, which had previously been the foundation of the Indians' whole existence, quite suddenly and dramatically became the property of the crowned heads of Spain. In turn, the monarchs of Spain gave grants of land to favorite Spaniards, who proceeded to enslave the Indians to work on the land.

In the course of the next few decades, the Spaniards embarked on a series of explorations and "discoveries" using the islands in the Caribbean as their base of operations. The initial settlements on the mainland—of North, Central and

Christopher Columbus pleading his cause at
the court of Ferdinand and Isabella.

South America—were made by explorers and adventurers who set out from Hispaniola (modern Haiti and the Dominican Republic) or from Cuba. With every new *entrada,* as each new expeditionary venture into strange land was called, the legal-minded Spaniards justified their forceful seizure of new lands. In 1512 a law was passed in Spain which stated that the Spaniards had to read to each new group of Indians that they might encounter a document called the *Requerimiento,* the Requirement.

It boggles the imagination to conceive of reading a document in *Spanish* to strange Indians in a strange territory. Even if the Requirement was read in the native tongue—as on occasion it was—the matter remains no less absurd considering the nature of its contents and the intruders' intentions. The Requirement outlined Genesis—how the Lord created the earth and Adam and Eve, *etc.*; proceeded to explain how Catholicism, the only true religion, came about; told how the Lord named St. Peter to judge and govern all mankind; said that a contemporary Pope had donated these lands to the monarchs of Spain; and declared that all the inhabitants were automatically vassals of Spanish lords and obliged to obey them. The final paragraph, quoted here in full, emphasizes the justness of the Spaniards' peculiar conduct:

> But if you do not do this [obey and cooperate] or if you maliciously delay in doing it, I certify to you that with the help of God we shall forcefully enter into your country and shall make war against you in all ways and manners that we can, and shall subject you to the yoke and obedience of the Church and of their highnesses; we shall take you and your wives and your children and shall make slaves of them, and as such shall sell and dispose of them as their highnesses may command; and we shall take away your goods and shall do

to you all the harm and damage that we can, as to vassals who do not obey and refuse to receive their lord and resist and contradict him; and we protest that the deaths and losses which shall accrue from this are your fault, and not that of their highnesses, or ours, or of these soldiers who come with us. And that we have said this to you and made this Requirement we request the notary here present to give us his testimony in writing, and we ask the rest who are present that they should be witnesses of this Requirement.

Even if such information were intelligible to the Indians it is doubtful that they would have appreciated having it. Undoubtedly it was of comfort to the invaders, whose consciences were then clear that what they were about to do— kill, steal and enslave—was legal and holy, sanctioned by the monarchs of Spain and by the Church.

On record are some ludicrous accounts attending the reading of the Requirement. One Spanish captain reported that he weighed anchor off a strange coast and, not knowing whether or not there were Indians present, and if there were, whether they might be hostile, he had one of his men on deck face the land and read the Requirement into the air. On another occasion, a group of Spaniards was trekking through strange land. The usual precautionary military tactic of deploying scouts ahead of the main body was rewarded with the report that about two miles further down the trail was an Indian village. If the inhabitants should be hostile, the leader reasoned, it would be well advised to take them by surprise. How then was the reading of the Requirement to be executed? The resourceful commander had one of his men face the distant village, and, in the dead of night, very quietly read the eight hundred word document. Having fulfilled the letter of the law, the Spaniards then attacked the village.

The great conquistador, Hernán Cortés, conqueror of Mexico, on at least one occasion had the Requirement read through an interpreter so that he might "act with entire regard to justice, and in obedience to the instructions of the Royal Council." Cortés and his men had weighed anchor at the mouth of a shallow river, Río de Tabasco, and noted that many menacing Indians were spread out on one bank

of the river, as well as in canoes along the shore. Cortés sent one detachment of about a hundred men to land at a point lower downstream while he undertook to lead the main body of his soldiers in a frontal assault across the stream. Before actually commencing hostilities, Cortés had

A contemporary Indian version of Cortés marching into the interior of Mexico. (From the sixteenth century Mexican Codex)

the Requirement read. The Indians responded with defiant shouts and a hail of arrows. The slaughter that followed was brief, the survivors were enslaved, their possessions seized, and their town and the surrounding land claimed for the crown. And, from the standpoint of the invader, it was both legal and moral. This was the standard practice to be repeated over and over again until the lands of the New World were appropriated by white, Christian Spaniards.

Cortés—blond, bearded, courageous, adventurous—was a Spanish nobleman who had lived in the Indies since 1504 and had participated in the conquest of Cuba. In 1519 he commanded an expedition to explore and conquer an unknown area on the continent where, it was reported, there were many Indians and much gold. With six hundred soldiers, eighteen horses and a few cannon, Cortés, in the course of two years, was able to defeat and enslave *millions* of Indians in a territory several times the size of Spain.

Of the many factors which accounted for Cortés' extraordinary success, the key one was the discord and hatred that existed among the many Indian tribes that inhabited Mexico. There is no doubt that the superiority of Spanish weapons, the fear inspired by horses—the first that the Indians had ever seen—the general Aztec belief that the blond, bearded Cortés was a god who, tradition said, was returning after many centuries, all these were important contributory factors. But six hundred men, no matter how brave and no matter how superior their arms, could not have subdued several million Indians if the Indians had been united. At the time of the arrival of the Europeans, the many Indian tribes were living in a loose confederation headed by the Aztecs. The center was located in what is now Mexico City, but the confederation extended throughout the Valley of Mexico and beyond.

After the conquest of Mexico, there was a great deal of intermarriage—legal and otherwise—between Spaniards and Indians, so that in time a large percentage of the population was *mestizo,* descendants of unions between Europeans and Indians.

When Cortés entered Mexico in 1519, the Aztecs had been head of a confederation of Indian tribes for about two hundred years. Their civilization has been compared with the glories of ancient Egypt. They had cities with all that that concept entails: public and private buildings and avenues; a division of labor including a ruling elite of warriors and priests as well as farmers, merchants, artisans and slaves. They practiced a complex religion with old traditions

A copy of an Indian drawing showing Moctezuma (center) facing Cortés and his Indian mistress, Doña Marina. Tenochtitlán was the name of the Aztec capital which is now Mexico City.

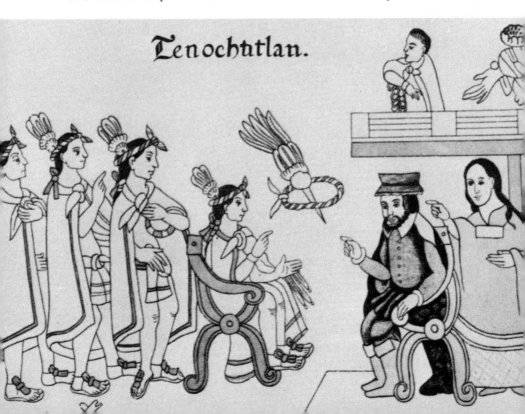

Tenochtitlan.

and rites, many of which were strikingly similar to those of Christianity. They had a system of writing with which they recorded their history and kept records. They wrote poetry. They possessed a highly developed technology which was evident in their engineering, in the magnificent architecture of their public buildings and the palace of the emperor. They had metallurgical skills. Craftsmanship of the highest order was exhibited in their works of art, sculptures, jewelry, dyeing, weaving, feather ornaments, silver and gold pieces. Farmers employed excellent systems of irrigation and had a thorough knowledge of the seasons. A calendar system equaling, if not surpassing, that of Europe showed considerable knowledge of astronomy and mathematics. Extensive trade was a normal daily practice and, while mostly internal, there was limited intercourse with their closest neighbors. The main market place near the capital astonished the Spaniards. Bernal Díaz del Castillo, one of Cortés' captains, wrote enthusiastically that the market place was larger than any he had seen in Spain. He also said that it had a great profusion of merchandise, was operated most efficiently, and had its own open courts of justice for dealing with problems right on the spot.

This magnificent civilization and neighboring ones as well were ripe for the plundering conquerors from the Old World. The Spaniards destroyed a great deal, yet they preserved much. During the past fifty years archaeologists and historians have uncovered  a seemingly limitless treasure of the glories of the ancient Mexican past.

The Spaniards borrowed much from the Indians. Three Indian foods affected the eating habits of Europe: the potato, corn and chocolate. Some other Indian foods and agricultural products include: beans (several varieties unknown to the Old World), chili, manioc, pumpkins, squash, turkey, a wide variety of fruits, dozens of herbs and medicinal plants.

Other aspects of Indian culture, especially arts and crafts, were adapted by their conquerors and subsequently by other peoples who came to the Americas. There are many reasons to justify the great pride that Mexican-Americans have in their Indian heritage.

When Cortés came, he found ready allies among those Indians who resented their enslavement and exploitation by the Aztecs. The Spanish conquest, therefore, was also a sort of civil war in which both sides lost to the foreign conqueror, who took everything.

The Aztec emperor, Moctezuma, had chosen to yield to the Spaniards. However another Aztec chieftain, Cuauhté-moc, led a revolt against his emperor and the Spaniards. Many thousands were killed in the course of prolonged fighting before the Spaniards and their allies were able to defeat the rebels. Today, in all Mexico there is no monument or other memorial to Moctezuma; there are several, including a most beautiful statue on the famous Paseo de la Reforma in Mexico City, of Cuauhtémoc. This is one example of the contradictory character of the Mexican-American heritage. On the one hand, acknowledgement of Spanish ancestry including pride in the heroic exploits of Cortés and his brave followers; on the other, acknowledgement of the courage of an Indian who chose to die rather than become a humble subject of a foreign power. The confusion is further compounded by the knowledge that the Aztecs were the hated enslavers and exploiters of other Indians.

After gaining the Aztec lands, the Spaniards moved out of the Valley of Mexico to conquer a vast territory which included what is now Mexico and the five republics of Central America, and the border regions to the north of what

The monument, in Mexico City, to Cuauhtémoc,
the Aztec leader who fought Cortés. There is
no monument in Mexico to the Aztec ruler,
Moctezuma, who surrendered to the Spanish
invaders.

are now California, Arizona, New Mexico, Utah, Colorado, Nevada and Texas. The whole was named New Spain and henceforth was to be a major part of the great Spanish overseas empire.

In New Spain the Spaniards found three things which fulfilled their fondest hopes: extensive, fertile land; an indigenous population to become the "hewers of wood and drawers of water"; and precious metals.

All the land now, in theory, belonged personally to the Spanish monarch, who could dispose of it as he saw fit. One way was to grant portions as rewards for meritorious service. Cortés was named Marqués of Oaxaca, lord of a valley of 25,000 square miles and, going along with this grant, or *encomienda,* were the 100,000 Indians living in the area; henceforth these Indians were required to labor or to pay tribute to their new master. Other Spaniards similarly were granted *encomiendas,* varying in size from a few acres to hundreds of thousands.

Eventually all the land was so divided, with some individuals becoming lords, *hacendados,* of great estates, *haciendas,* on which the Indians toiled as slaves.

When, in 1542, the enslavement of Indians was declared illegal, the colonists found subterfuges to exploit the Indians with little or no pay. A principal method was the system of peonage. A free Indian was employed on a ranch or farm for a pay so low that he had to borrow from his master. The conditions of borrowing were so onerous that it was impossible for a peon to rid himself of the debt. He, and his family, were bound interminably. Even after his death, his children were held legally responsible for the intolerable burden, thereby guaranteeing their continued enslavement.

Indians were drafted periodically into forced labor for the building of roads, canals, and other public works and,

A late nineteenth century artist's version of
the famous Mission Dolores in San Francisco.

until the mid-eighteenth century, even into factories and
mines. A few Indians who lived in inaccessible areas in
jungles and in some mountain regions escaped exploitation
by the Spaniards.

Agriculture was a synthesis of the cultures of the Old and

New Worlds. The Spaniards combined their skills with those of the Indians. They borrowed much; they contributed more. The Spaniards brought to the New World all the citrus fruits, rice, coffee, sugar cane; all the domesticated livestock —chickens, ducks, geese, sheep, cattle, horses, hogs; the cereals—oats, rye, barley and wheat. Those cereals were more important to the newcomers than to the Indians who relied upon maize, a staple to be eaten in a variety of ways: *tortillas,* corn on the cob, cornmeal, *enchiladas, tacos,* and so on.

Where there is little rain the farmer somehow must supply water to his fields. Irrigation was an indispensable concomitant of much of agriculture in New Spain and especially in the border regions, where so much of the land was semi-arid. During the centuries-long occupation of the Iberian peninsula by the Moors, the most advanced methods of irrigation were instituted, and continued thereafter by the Spaniards. In the New World, Indians had efficient irrigation methods which were further improved by their conquerors. When the colonists of the United States started to pour into the Southwest, they learned and used the irrigation techniques of the Spanish-speaking inhabitants.

Although they came to the New World for several reasons, gold was uppermost in the fevered imaginations of Spaniards. GOLD! With GOLD, wrote Columbus, one could even get souls into Paradise! When gold and silver were pouring into Europe from the mines exploited by the Spaniards, Shakespeare, in his play *Timon of Athens,* written in 1607, has the principal character exclaim:

> Gold? yellow, glittering, precious gold?
> Thus much of this will make black white, foul fair,
> Wrong, right, base noble, old young, coward valiant.
> Ha, you gods! why this? what this, you gods? Why, this
> Will lug your priests and servants from your sides,
> Pluck stout men's pillow from below their heads;
> This yellow slave
> Will knit and break religions; bless the accursed;
> Make the hoar leprosy adored; place thieves,
> And give them title, knee and approbation
> With senators on the bench . . .

Men, even in modern times, impute to a metal supernatural qualities which give the possessor superhuman power. Rational men deride superstitious individuals who assume that some natural object—like a four-leaf clover—possesses some nonnatural power; yet those same reasoning men, and nations, have a similar belief about gold.

The Indians, before Columbus arrived, had many superstitions, but none about gold and silver. These metals were used for adornment, decoration and even in dental and surgical practices. After seizing the gold and silver that had been accumulated by the Indians over centuries, the Spaniards began to exploit the old Indian mines and, after considerable prospecting, found and developed new, superior ones.

Spectacularly large deposits of silver were found in the sixteenth and seventeenth centuries in Guanajuato, San Luis Potosí and Zacatecas. By the end of the seventeenth century New Spain was the leading producer of precious metals in colonial America. Mining techniques were perfected, and during the last third of the eighteenth century the Spanish kings commissioned European experts to introduce the very latest reforms in the mines of the New World. The experts did indeed introduce many improvements but, curiously enough, found that the Mexican *patio* method of extracting the silver from the poorer ores found in Mexico was superior to the accepted European technique applied to richer ores. The great German scientist, Baron Alexander von Humboldt, lectured at the famous School of Mines in Mexico City. After visiting universities in the United States, Humboldt remarked: "No city of the new continent, without excepting those of the United States, can display such great and solid scientific establishments as the capital of New Spain. I shall content myself here with naming the School of Mines . . . the Botanic Garden; and the Academy of Painting and Sculpture. . . ." Later in the same century, American miners in California, Colorado, Arizona and New Mexico were to take advantage of the contributions made by the Mexicans.

The last two references indicate that the Mexicans made contributions other than in mundane practical matters. Humboldt comments that at the Academy of Painting and Sculpture there had been collected, at great expense, casts of the great masterpieces of sculpture found in Europe. Some steps were taken to preserve the magnificent sculptures of the Aztecs. And, Mexicans were beginning to produce their own works. A professor of sculpture, a Señor Tolsa, cast an equestrian statue of King Charles IV which still draws admiring looks from those who pass by its beautiful stand in one of the *glorietas* (traffic circles) in Mexico City. Classes were conducted free at the Academy. Humboldt commented:

> The academy labours successfully to introduce among the artisans a taste for elegance and beautiful forms. Large rooms, well lighted by Argand's lamps, contain every evening some hundreds of young people, of whom some draw from relievo or living models, while others copy drawings of furniture, chandeliers, or other ornaments in bronze. In this assemblage (and this is very remarkable in the midst of a country where the prejudices of the nobility against the castes are so inveterate) rank, colour, and race is confounded; we see the Indian and the mestizo sitting beside the white, and the son of a poor artisan in emulation with the children of the great lords of the country. It is a consolation to observe, that under every zone the cultivation of science and art establishes a certain equality among men, and obliterates for a time, at least,

all those petty passions of which the effects are so prejudicial to social happiness.

One feels called upon to comment that it is still the unhappy fact that the prejudices described by Humboldt have proliferated and that it is only in the arts, and to a lesser degree in sports and in the sciences, that distinctions of skin color, class and caste have become meaningless.

Important strides in the study of the physical sciences were made in New Spain. It was Humboldt's sophisticated opinion that "No European government has sacrificed greater sums to advance the knowledge of the vegetable kingdom than the Spanish government." Located within the grounds of the viceroy's palace was a botanical garden where the Mexican scholar, Professor Vicente Cervantes, conducted well-attended courses. The School of Mines possessed a chemical laboratory, a geological collection and a physics laboratory containing the most advanced instruments. Andrés del Rio, a Mexican, composed one of the finest treatises on mineralogy, and discovered the metal vanadium. José Antonio Alzate y Ramírez wrote extensively on physics, astronomy and biology in *The Literary Gazette,* a periodical devoted—despite its title—to the physical sciences.

*God,* Gold and Glory! For some who came to the New World, the emphasis was on God. Of all the Spanish-Mexican institutions, the most enduring, and the one with a powerful influence that has extended right to the present, is the Catholic Church. Friars were present on Columbus' voyages, and today priests play a significant role in the current Chicano movement. The people of the American Southwest have lived through many political, social and economic

An imaginative Spanish artist's portrayal of
Cortés and his troops fighting in Tenochtitlán.

changes but the religion of the majority of the Spanish-speaking segment remains Catholic.

At first the clergymen who came to the New World were missionaries of the regular, or monastic orders—Jesuits, Franciscans, Dominicans and several others. As the colonial period wore on, the Church sent secular clergy * who gradually replaced the regular orders in numbers and in importance.

Besides carrying out the usual religious duties, the missionaries bore the very special burden of converting millions of Indians. Since there were so many to be converted and relatively so few clergy, it was often the case that conversion would take place *en masse*. Sometimes the formality bordered on the ludicrous; bishops sprinkled some drops of holy water over a hushed assemblage of several hundred Indians and pronounced them Christian, and then later complained of having thus laboriously baptized thousands of Indians in one day. Such practices were condemned by the more pious and dedicated, who took their task of conversion more seriously.

Earnestness and piety were not the marks of all friars and nuns. The historian should not generalize in one direction or the other, wholly praising or condemning the Church. The records are as filled with the actions of those who performed nobly and heroically as they are with those whose deeds brought shame and degradation to the cloth. There are villains and heroes in all professions and institutions.

How effective was the Church in making practicing Christians of the pagan Indians? Two hundred and seventy-five years after the Conquest almost all of the Indians had

---

* Secular clergy refers to all those religious functionaries who are not members of one of the monastic orders.

been converted. But Baron von Humboldt noted: "The natives know nothing of religion but the exterior forms of worship. Fond of whatever is connected with a prescribed order of ceremonies, they find in the Christian religion particular enjoyments. . . ."

And the viceroy Revillagigedo II reported: "What is regrettable is that such great expenditure, such labors and zeal, and so many wise measures taken at all times for this purpose [*i.e.*, religious understanding], have not produced the desired result, and the Indians are still very ignorant and uncultured in religious matters."

It was not only laymen like Humboldt and Revillagigedo who made such observations, but on occasion bishops communicating with their superiors in Madrid or Rome also noted that the religious understanding of converted Indians was woefully lacking.

The clergy also fulfilled functions other than religious. All education, from infancy through University, was in the exclusive hands of the Church. In the matter of education, the Jesuit order was most influential; however all the orders were zealous in establishing schools for the elementary religious education of the Indians.

Moral standards of the Indians were different from those of the Spaniards, and the attempts to change them were seldom successful. For example, most Indians practiced polygamy and while they may have accepted on faith the monogamous standard of the European, they did not carry it out in practice. Nor were matters helped by Spaniards openly violating their own ethical principles or by the examples set by some members of the clergy, who openly violated their vows of chastity. Scandalous conduct by laymen aroused the indignation of honest clergymen who were put in the very difficult position of having to answer for the outrageous conduct of their fellow countrymen.

At the same time, some clergymen found Gold to be more appealing than God. So covetous were some men of the cloth that they abandoned the Church altogether and in a few cases accumulated enough wealth to retire, returning to Spain to enjoy their riches. The first viceroy to New Spain wrote, in 1550: "The clergy who come to these parts are wicked and motivated by self-interest. If it were not for what His Majesty has commanded, and for baptism, the Indians would be better off without them so far as other things are concerned. . . . This is in general, because some priests are good as individuals." Bishop Zumárraga complained that the clergy were ignorant, immoral and corrupt. A succession of viceroys reported that the priests were guilty of concubinage, luxurious living, theft of money, and violation of Church rules.

Since the Church had a monopoly on educational institutions, it exercised considerable intellectual control. Catholicism was the official religion, and no other was tolerated, so the Church enjoyed complete control over private and public morals. It had considerable weight in political affairs. A strict censorship made it difficult even for the elite to receive and read books condemned by the Church.

The Holy Inquisition, whose official aims were to eliminate heresy and punish apostates and specified evildoers, censored all reading matter and all public entertainments. It became a scourge, dreaded and feared by everyone. From its inception in the New World in 1569 until its abolition in 1813, it was responsible for the imprisonment of tens of thousands, the torture of thousands, the burning at the stake of hundreds. Jews, and individuals charged with being Jews or with being over-friendly to Jews, were hounded, tortured and their wealth sequestered. While it is true that relatively few people were directly victimized by the Inquisition, the entire community felt harassed, living in constant fear of being subjected to visitation from the Holy Office. It was generally known that once accused, very, very few were declared innocent. The abolition of this medieval horror in 1813 was long overdue and universally welcomed.

The most severe critics of the Church acknowledge many positive contributions. Many clerics suffered martyrdom in the course of sincere efforts to help the Indians. Missionaries taught Indians various crafts; they learned the languages of the Indians and then wrote grammars and dictionaries as well as leaving for posterity a number of historical books of great interest and importance. Missionaries were explorers, scientists and map makers. Under their guidance, besides building missions, convents, monasteries and churches, the Indians helped to construct hospitals and schools. Devout fathers often defended the Indians against the worst abuses of the Spanish laymen. It was a Dominican friar, later to become a bishop, Bartolomé de las Casas, who because of his selfless devotion to the Indians, became known, and is still remembered, as the "Apostle of the Indians." It was Las Casas who fought against the monarchy, the leadership of the Church and against the aristocrats in the New World in order to obtain laws abolishing the legal enslavement of the Indians.

The legal battle was won in 1542 with the passage of laws forbidding the enslavement of the Indians. However the laws were more broken than carried out. Laymen were not alone in violating these laws; the Church's many properties were worked on by Indians whose condition remained virtual slavery. One of the most valuable properties of the powerful Jesuit order, before it was expelled in 1767, was in the form of slaves. This included not just Indians, but

Blacks as well. The Apostle of the Indians, overlooked the plight of the black man, and in his struggles to defend the Indians, was perfectly willing to replace Indian workers with black African slave labor. In later years, Las Casas acknowledged his error in not fighting for the dignity of all human beings.

Of the few clerics in the colonial period who attacked the institution of slavery consistently and earnestly, Sor Juana Inés de la Cruz must be singled out. This nun (1651-1695) was known in New Spain as the Tenth Muse. She had many interests and many talents, the greatest of which was evidenced in the "curious light music" of her poetry. Her dedication to religion did not interfere with her interest in secular learning. She was an eloquent defender—one of the very earliest—of the rights of women to education and intellectual activity. And, she was splendid in her indignant criticism of the enslavement of Indians and Blacks. Unfortunately the Sor Juanas were few and far between, lonely voices of humanitarianism either in or outside of the Church.

The Church attained great economic power in the course of the centuries of colonial rule. It acquired land (becoming the largest landowner in Spanish America), livestock, warehouses, factories, mines, city real estate, plantations and a variety of other commercial enterprises. All in all, the Church was the most powerful single political, social and economic force in the colonies.

By the end of the colonial period, New Spain had about

Bartolomé de las Casas. At first a conquistador, then a priest and finally Bishop of Chiapas. For his efforts on behalf of the American Indians he became known as the "Apostle of the Indians."

seven million people, of which about one million were white. Approximately one half of the rest were Indian and the others were mixtures of Spaniard, Indian and Black. That there were so few whites is due mostly to Spain's immigration policy, which excluded all foreigners from her possessions in the New World. There were a few exceptions— some English, French and Germans, who had managed to enter and stay permanently in New Spain. The great majority, then, were Indian and *mestizo*.

In the course of three hundred years, the Spaniards had conquered and settled a vast domain several times larger than Spain herself. The colonies endured far longer than those of any of the other European powers who had expanded in the New World.

While New Spain was a Spanish colony, it developed along paths different from the mother country. The language, the Church, economic and political institutions were Spanish, but all were considerably modified by the new environment, and by the merging of Spanish and Indian cultures to become something different—Mexican. The Mexican language is as different from Spanish as American is from English. The Spanish Roman Catholic Church was influenced by Indian customs. The sheep and cattle raising of Spain were transformed into great new industries in New Spain where they underwent many changes. Mexican life after three hundred years of Spanish colonization was considerably different from Spanish life.

As New Spain differed from Spain, so did its various parts. The borderlands in the north, or the American Southwest, were conquered, settled and developed differently than the central portion, Mexico.

Ah, Indians, ah, you dogs of
the worst breed that the sun
warms !
Diego de Vargas

## CHAPTER III
# Conquest of the Southwest

IN MOST HOLLYWOOD "WESTERNS," INDIANS LOOK AND BE-
have pretty much alike. There are some "good" Indians; they
side with the Americans. Most are "bad" Indians; they fight,
occasionally bravely, often stupidly against the heroes.
Movie Indians are caricatures of people.

The fact of the matter is that there was a great variety of
Indians, all of whom differed considerably in physical ap-
pearance and cultural development. At the time of the discovery of the New World, there were hundreds of tribes,
speaking hundreds of languages, and having many different
customs. Some were extremely warlike, some were canni-
bals, some were quite peaceful. Their development varied
from the lowest stages of barbarism—extremely primitive
cultural groups—to highly developed civilizations whose
accomplishments astonished the invading Spaniards.

In the area of what is now the southwestern part of the
United States—from Texas in the east to California on the
west—the Spaniards encountered dozens of tribes. Some,

were simple food gatherers using the most elementary tools and weapons such as sticks and stones. Others, more sophisticated, employed bows and arrows, and hunted large game, trapped fur bearing animals, and fished. Some, like the Pueblo Indians, had graduated from a simple nomadic existence to having permanent homes, and villages; they were farmers and supplemented their living by hunting.

The first Spaniards to meet any of these Indians of the Southwest were Alvar Núñez Cabeza de Vaca and three companions, one of whom was a Moorish slave named Estevanico, or Estevan. They were the survivors of a Spanish expedition of 580 men, led by Pánfilo de Narváez, who had landed on the west coast of Florida in 1528. These four men reached Mexico after surviving extraordinary hardships for eight interminable years of wandering along the Gulf coast from western Florida to Texas. During those eight years the four strangers enjoyed the cordial friendship of some tribes, and suffered the hostility of others. For a considerable time they were the captives of primitive Indians, and like them, the four went naked, lived on roots, berries, reptiles, insects and shellfish which were caught with the bare hands.

Fortunately for the foreigners, most of the Indians were friendly. Cabeza de Vaca and the slave gained a reputation for being medicine men capable of accomplishing miracles. That reputation, plus the curiosity of the Indians on seeing a black man for the first time made it possible for the four to survive. They were forced to live as the Indians did and traveled with them when it suited their Indian hosts' needs or fancy. In gratitude for the curing powers of Cabeza and Estevanico, the Indians were eventually kind enough to escort the four guests from place to place, and to turn them over to other friendly tribes, thus aiding them in their westerly journey toward Mexico.

Cabeza's privations and experiences had profound effects. He wrote:

> Months went by as in a dream. The nerve of vision no longer rendered plausible that European world of which we had been a part. That world grew fantastic; and fantastic our countrymen there. We ourselves were only too real. From lack of clothing we had big sores and deep skin fissures on our backs and shoulders, and it hurt us to carry the hides we slept in. And it hurt us to find firewood among the cactus. My thighs and arms bled so much I stood it only by remembering—and yet whom or what did I remember? Was it a Person—was it a quality of life—was it an emotion? . . .

He vowed that he would "teach the world how to conquer by gentleness, not by slaughter," for he had been so impressed with the kindness of the Indians.

On the other hand, he was sharply critical of the behavior of the Spanish conquerors, expressing his indignation that "Christians should be so wicked . . . ." This anger was aroused at the very moment of his first contact with the Spaniards who rescued him near the Yaqui River. His fellow Christians found him while they were engaged in a slave-hunting expedition. Here is Cabeza's account of his recontact with civilized men:

> Our countrymen, these slave catchers, were startled when they saw us approaching. Yet almost with their first words they began to recite their troubles. For many days they had been unable to find Indians to capture. They did not know what to do, and were on the point of starvation. The idea of enslaving our Indians occurred to them in due course, and they were vexed at us for preventing it. They had their interpreter make a fine speech. He told our Indians that we were as a matter of fact Christians too, but had gone astray for a

The Mission of San Diego de Alcalá in
California.

long while, and were people of no luck and little heart. Our
Indians considered this point of view. They answered that the
real Christians apparently lied, that we could not possibly be
Christians. For we appeared out of sunrise, they out of sun-
set; we cured the sick; while they killed even the healthy; we
went naked and barefoot, while they wore clothes, and rode
horseback and stuck people with lances; we asked for nothing

and gave away all we were given, while they never gave anybody anything and had no other aim than to steal.

And, Cabeza added, it was most difficult for him to face the Spanish gentleman which he himself had once been.

After reaching Mexico City, the stories related by Cabeza to Viceroy Mendoza and his fellow courtiers confirmed preexisting myths of gold and treasure and staggered the imagination of the Spaniards. One of the most persistent myths that had been circulating for several decades concerned an imaginary land wherein were seven fabled cities brimming over with gold and diamonds and pearls. Cabeza reported that he had seen some evidence of gold and that he had been informed by several Indians that there were Indians to the north who lived in houses, engaged in farming, and were rich in gold and jewels. While Cabeza had not been to the area, the descriptions were sufficiently vivid to lead him, and his greedy listeners, to believe any extravagances.

One may imagine that, with the difficulties of understanding Indian languages, and fired by an obsession with gold, Cabeza was easily persuaded that tremendous wealth awaited any European who would be daring enough to explore the north. And, possibly, to naked Indian nomads, sedentary people who lived in a few adobe houses, and who wore clothes constituted a large, and possibly dangerous, population. Their vague oral descriptions, accompanied by hand signs, of metal trinkets and stones, probably were translated by Cabeza and his companions to mean turquoises, emeralds, pearls, gold, copper and so on. To the Indian "many" might have meant something more than fifty; whereas to a European "many" might have meant something more than 50,000.

Stimulated by the realistic and highly imaginative accounts of the four wanderers, Mendoza decided to outfit an expedition to ascertain the truth of Cabeza de Vaca's reports. The command of the expedition was entrusted to Francisco de Coronado, only recently appointed to the governorship of a vast province in northern New Spain called New Galicia. However, the viceroy was not one to throw caution completely to the winds. Before launching a full fledged, and expensive expedition, he advised Coronado to send out first a relatively small exploratory group to be headed by the Franciscan friar, Marcos de Niza.

In 1539, Fray Marcos began the trek northward into New Mexico and Arizona. He was aided by the black man, Estevanico, who had acquired invaluable experience during the eight years he had spent with the Indians. Estevanico led an advance party and sent back encouraging reports to the timid friar who was cautiously ensconced in an Indian village. One enthusiastic report said that there was a vast country in the north in which there were seven cities, the most important of which was Cíbola. In it were large houses constructed of stone and lime, many of which were several stories high with doorways ornamented with turquoises. After fifteen days of tortuous marching to the northern edge of the Arizona desert, Fray Marcos was informed that Estevanico had been killed, victim of his greed and lust for women, in Hawikuh, one of the pueblos of the Zuñi Indians. Any hope of friendly relations with the Zuñis—or Cíbolans as the Spaniards now called them—was ended. Fray Marcos forthwith departed for the safety of Mexico City.

His report to the viceroy was compounded of partial truths, exaggerations and fancifully embroidered lies. He alleged that he had seen a land "rich in gold, silver and other wealth." He described in detail the city of Cíbola, and that the houses "are of stone, terraced like those of Mexico. The cities were guarded with gates, and the people were very rich, the women even wearing belts of gold. In the country were silversmiths, blacksmiths, slaughterhouses, baths, sheep and partridges." Can you blame Cortés, at the time Marqués de la Valle, for calling the Franciscan a liar? Mendoza, however, swallowed the story, hook, line and sinker.

Coronado now led a full-scale expedition—250 horsemen, 70 infantrymen, 300 Indian allies, 1,000 Negro and Indian slaves—personally financed by himself and the viceroy, northward from Mexico. After great travail he reached Hawikuh. Far from being a great city "guarded by gates," Hawikuh was a small, squalid Zuñi pueblo, one of some eighty, inhabited by a total population of perhaps 16,000. The pueblo was a communal structure of houses made of stone or adobe, terraced in such a fashion that at the center it was six stories high. To reach the top, ladders were employed. No doors. No gold. No silver, pearls, turquoises. No baths. No slaughterhouses. No blacksmiths.

In the name of the King, and given the necessary blessing by the friars, Coronado gave battle to the Indians, quickly subdued them, and announced that henceforth the Cíbolans were subjects of the King of Spain!

The new subjects provided guides for the Spaniards who went on to conquer the neighboring Hopis, likewise pueblo-dwellers. The Hopis proffered a few gifts which were munificent in their eyes but were pitiable for the Spaniards. Mendoza and Coronado had not gone to such considerable expense and trouble to be satisfied with a few skins, nuts, and corn.

Coronado was not yet ready to give up. The dreams of great riches were too real, too overpowering. And so the army continued, eastward and northward. The Colorado River was reached by one group, and immediately claimed by the Spaniards. For the first time white men gazed upon the awesome splendors of the Grand Canyon. Many pueblos were seen, including that of the now famous Taos. Some Indians were friendly; many resisted only to succumb to the superior armaments of the Spanish conquerors.

Coronado's hopes were raised when he heard of a great country to the northeast. In it were many cities, the largest of which was Quivira, filled with gold and jewels. Off to Quivira! The Spaniards reached Kansas; they were the first white men to see the huge herds of buffalo that meant food, fuel, clothing and housing for the Indians of the plains. But they found no cities, no Quivira.

After a year and a half of marches through deserts, over mountains, across rivers and innumerable streams, and having found no gold, no pearls, no emeralds, nothing of what he had come for, a most disappointed and dispirited Coronado finally decided to return to Mexico. The myth of the Seven Cities of Cíbola had finally been laid to rest.

Yet there were some long lasting consequences to Coronado's unproductive journey. The Spaniards had introduced the horse to the Southwest. It is not known for sure whether the wild horses that subsequently inhabited the area came from stock introduced by Coronado or developed from later Spanish expeditions; both are highly probable. Furthermore, Coronado had brought back with him very intelligent reports about the inhabitants and the geography, and made a fairly accurate assessment of the natural resources of the immense area.

The disappointments of those early expeditions discouraged any new ones for a long time. Besides, the Spaniards were busy colonizing the vast area of Mexico proper. Rich silver mines were discovered and exploited. Sheep and cattle ranches were developed. The Church was busy baptizing and training millions of Indians in Christian ways. Governmental procedures were tried, changed, extended, to create a viable administration of the land and its people.

About forty years after Coronado's return, new expeditions set out to explore the northern frontiers. Several missionaries made unsuccessful *entradas* and paid for their daring with their lives. In 1582, a wealthy colonist, Antonio de Espejo, brought back definite proof that there were silver mines in the regions of western Arizona. But it was not until 1598 that the first permanent settlements were made in the area north of the Rio Grande. The man most responsible for that accomplishment was Juan de Oñate.

Oñate—proud, fearless, ruthless, and extremely ambitious —convinced the viceroy to grant him the privilege of exploring the borderlands, of "pacifying" the Indians there, and of founding a colony.

Oñate inherited ownership in one of the richest silver mines in the world, Zacatecas. At age fifty, when he set out on his expedition, he was one of the four richest men in New Spain; he had to be, for he financed solely out of his own resources an expedition which included four hundred men, women and children (the families had to be included since one of the principal aims was to establish permanent settlements); eighty-three wagons (*carretas*, the first wheeled vehicles ever seen by the Indians) and seven thousand cattle, the first permanent herd in what was to become the great cattle empire of the American Southwest.

At last success crowned the efforts of the Spanish conquistadores. Several permanent settlements were established; among the most famous were El Paso, San Juan, San Gabriel, and Santa Fe, which was to become the capital of the province.

It was Oñate who gave the name "Apache" to one large band of Indians. Apache was the Zuñi word for "enemy," as indeed the Apaches were. The Apache-Navajo had been pushed to the southwest by the Comanches, and at the time of the Spanish conquest were enemies to all—Indians and Spaniards. While the Apaches remained unsubdued, Oñate was able to conquer and enslave many thousands of Indians in New Mexico and Arizona.

Oñate's report to the viceroy supplied many additional

details of the land and its inhabitants. As his predecessors had done, he exaggerated in some measures. For example, he wrote of "the great wealth that the mineral lodes have begun to reveal, and the large number of them in the land. . . ." And further, he asserted "the certainty of the nearness of the South Sea [the Pacific], whose trade with Peru, New Spain, and China should not be underestimated, for with the passing of time it will be the source of profitable and continuous customs revenues because of its proximity to China. . . ."

Indians were enslaved or, in some cases, made into allies of the Spaniards. It was the much repeated pattern of the Spanish conquest as set by Cortés and his captains. The fiercer the resistance of the Indians, the more ruthless were their conquerors. Of the 3,000 Indians in the pueblo of Ácoma, only 600 were permitted to surrender; the rest, including women and children, were slaughtered for having dared to resist. In Oñate's report to the viceroy about the incident, he wrote, "As punishment for Ácoma's crime and its treason against His Majesty . . . and as a warning to the rest, I razed and burned it completely."

Oñate was made governor of the new territory, a post he held until 1607 when he was forced to resign. The viceroy was dissatisfied after receiving many reports about mistreatment of Indians and even of colonists and of soldiers. Probably the principal reason for the viceroy's discontent with Oñate was that the latter had misrepresented the mineral value of New Mexico.

During the next decades the process of settlement proceeded relatively slowly. Inducements for Spaniards and *criollos* (Creoles—people born in the New World and claiming European ancestry) for settling in the borderlands were not as great as within Mexico proper. Life in New Mexico in those early days was full of hardships, not the least of which was incessant warfare with the Indians. And, civil and religious leaders were constantly at odds with one another. However, it was the Indian who was the sorry victim and looked with growing contempt upon both representatives of imperial authority, religious and civil. The net result was the undermining of Spanish control over the Indians, most of whom were not too happy about being subjects of a foreign power in the first place, and who resented the forced acceptance of a new religion.

The civil-religious conflict served as a prologue to a civil war between the Indians and their foreign masters. Led by a medicine man, Popé, the Pueblo Indians revolted in 1680. The uprising had been carefully planned for five years. Although the Spaniards had some forewarning, the extensive character of the revolt caught them unprepared. Indians from every pueblo in the territory united under the mystic Popé. The pent-up hatred of the Indians exploded with such success that after about one month of fierce fighting, the burning of farms, houses and churches, and many deaths on both sides, all the surviving Spaniards withdrew to the other side of the Rio Grande. The revolt of the Pueblos remains to this day the most spectacular victory ever won by North American Indians against European invaders.

The Indians reverted to their original faith. The Spanish language was forbidden; everything Spanish that was not utilitarian was destroyed. The land of the pueblos was Indian again—for twelve years.

In California, as well as New Mexico, significant events were taking place.

The first Europeans to see California were Spaniards. Ten years after Cortés had established Spanish rule over

Mexico, he sent out maritime expeditions northward. The Bay of La Paz, at the southern tip of Lower California, was reached by two Spanish ships in 1533. The Indians killed the crews and the captains. In 1535, Cortés himself led an expedition of three ships, and set up a colony at La Paz. It had to be abandoned within a year because the colonists, failing to obtain supplies from Mexico, were unable to endure the severe hardships.

At about the same time that Coronado undertook his land expedition, Cortés sent another sea expedition of three vessels commanded by Francisco de Ulloa. He determined that Lower California was a peninsula and not, as had been mistakenly believed, an island. After reaching the mouth of the Colorado River, Ulloa sailed down the eastern shores of Lower California, went around the tip and continued northward along the western coast. This enterprise too ended in complete disaster; all the ships and their crews disappeared.

In 1540 Hernando de Alarcón, commander of a seaborne expedition that was to coordinate its activities with Coronado's main land operation, sailed up the Gulf, reached the Colorado River, and ascended its muddy waters some two hundred miles. Alarcón, then, probably was the first European to see any part of the land now called California.

However it was a Portuguese, Juan Rodríguez Cabrillo, serving the Spaniards, who explored the California coast in 1544. After Cabrillo's untimely death, his successor, Bartolomé Ferrelo, reached the Rogue River on the Oregon coast, laying the basis for Spain's claim to the area north of California.

For some years thereafter the Spanish officials ignored California, concentrating their energies on developing Mexico. Yet indirectly the California coast played a minor role in the development of Mexico, for starting in 1565 Spanish ships returning from the Philippines made California their first landfall. Captains and crews constantly pleaded with the authorities in Mexico to establish ports of call on the California coast to serve at least as temporary stop-overs after the long, hardship-filled voyage from Manila.

In 1577 the great English sea captain, Sir Francis Drake, commenced a series of highly successful raids along the Pacific coast and succeeded in sufficiently alarming the Mexican authorities. They established a few settlements, and carried out some explorations, but extensive colonization was not to take place until the eighteenth century.

**Reconquest of New Mexico** After having been driven below the Rio Grande, Spain temporarily abandoned her attempt to develop the northern territory. A number of military forays in the 1680's into the area accomplished little of permanent value other than to reinforce the Indians' determination to resist and to keep the white man out.

From the moment in 1691 when Diego de Vargas Zapata y Luján de León assumed the duties of governor, he was determined to reconquer New Mexico for the crown and to gratify his personal ambition.

Vargas, close to fifty years old, proved to be capable, fearless and ruthless—a combination of traits found in so many Spanish conquerors. After first quieting rebellious Indians along the lower Rio Grande, Vargas headed a small force of about one hundred and ten Spanish soldiers and a hundred or so Indian allies. In September of 1692, after having marched through several deserted pueblos, the group reached Santa Fe. The Tano Indians were living in the town, occupying buildings which had formerly been the governor's palace, other royal homes and the private homes of the earlier Spanish colonists.

In this instance there was no bloodshed. After enduring a brief siege, the Tanos surrendered and passively accepted the usual Catholic formalities. The priests gave absolution and baptized all those children that had been born since the revolt twelve years before. This was pretty much the pattern that evolved as pueblo after pueblo succumbed to the indomitable Vargas.

Even the Hopis, who had been the most defiant of the Pueblo Indians, submitted. At a critical moment when the Hopis were threatening to resist, the mounted Vargas shouted:

> Ah, Indians, ah, you dogs of the worst breed that the sun warms! Do you think that my tolerance is owing to fear of your numbers and arms? Pity is what I have had for you in not killing you, for by a single threat on my part, you would all perish! . . . Kneel, kneel at once before I consume you all with the fires of my indignation!"

If the Hopis did not understand the flowery Spanish, apparently they gathered its import, for they were completely cowed. Vargas' fiery spirit convinced them, combined undoubtedly with the Hopis' memories of the horrible might of the Spaniards' horses, armor, steel swords, arquebuses and cannons.

Not so the Apaches. Those stalwart warriors persisted in harassing Vargas, even daring to attack the soldiers on the march. Such hostile intransigency of the few Apaches did not prevent Vargas from completing his task of conquest, a task made possible partly because the Pueblo Indians were no longer united as they had been under Popé.

Vargas returned to his original base at El Paso del Norte where he spent several months recruiting a larger army as well as gathering a large number of would-be settlers and seventeen friars. This contingent returned to Santa Fe in December of 1693, but instead of being able to commence the arduous task of peaceful resettlement, the Spaniards were unexpectedly confronted with Tanos Indians once again turned hostile.

A brief battle ended in a Spanish victory. Sixty-nine warriors were condemned to death, not for having resisted the white man but for having smashed holy images and for having uttered blasphemies like the shouted challenge that the Devil could do more for them than God or María. The surviving Indians were distributed among the colonists as slaves. Santa Fe was restored as the capital of the province.

Much remained to be done. One town, described as a capital, does not constitute a province. Other settlements had to be established, and to do so required that Vargas subdue Indian tribes that were still in a state of rebellion or which might rebel. Besides, any future settlements would be meaningful only if a labor supply—Indians—could be guaranteed. Vargas set out immediately to pacify and conquer.

Some Indians were friendly, some hostile. Victories were interspersed with occasional defeats. Yet, even victories were sometimes obtained at great cost, as in the instance of the battle at the Tunyo mesa, home of the thunder gods (now called Black Butte), where the Pueblo Indians took advantage of the natural volcanic fortifications. The Spanish victory was short-lived, for the Indians who had been compelled to return to their pueblos after the defeat at Tunyo, rose in revolt, killed missionaries and other Spaniards, and fled to the mountains.

For the next five years Vargas was busy fighting, gaining temporary successes only to face a revitalized Indian tribe that would rather fight than submit. Captured Indians were variously treated; some were given absolution and then shot;

some committed suicide; some were sold into slavery; some returned to live in their pueblos. The Apaches, and the even fiercer Comanches, never gave in.

The majority was finally reduced to servitude. By 1700, New Mexico was firmly in the hands of the Spaniards. Settlement in earnest could proceed.

California  In their drive to the northwest the Spaniards were concerned not only with New Mexico, but, as we have already seen, with California. Long after Vizcaíno's trip, explorations were made by sea and by land. By land, from northern Sonora, the Spaniards had to deal with unfriendly Indians and with desert wastes just beyond the Colorado River. To avoid the desert meant crossing two ranges of mountains and a number of streams and rivers before reaching the desired goal of the southern California coast.

One of the most prominent figures in the early expansion to the northwest, the one who was most responsible for laying the groundwork for the later successes, was the Jesuit friar Eusebio Francisco Kino. An Italian Swiss, born in 1644, he entered the order of the Society of Jesus at age twenty-one and was a particularly outstanding scholar during his period of training in southern Germany. At age twenty-five, Kino volunteered to serve as a missionary in the New World.

Kino combined zeal and ability in his vocation as missionary and in his multiple talents as an explorer, map maker, astronomer, and cattle raiser. He explored and worked in the area known as Pimería Alta—northern Sonora and southern Arizona—and part of Lower California. He carried out more than forty expeditions, founded twenty-nine missions, baptized several thousand Indians, instructed the Indians in crafts, made remarkably accurate maps, and developed a number of cattle ranches. Throughout all these labors, he remained a dedicated, pious, humble servant of the Indians, who had found very few white men they could trust. Kino's sincerity and completely unselfish devotion won their undying loyalty. He died among the Indians, at age 67, on the simple bed that had been his custom to use—two calf-skins for a mattress, two blankets, and a pack-saddle for a pillow.

Father Kino's extensive explorations had led him to the conclusive proof that Baja California was not an island, verifying previous estimates, and he urged that an overland route could be found from Sonora to upper California. He added his influential voice to the growing demand that ports of call be established on the upper California coast. But Spain and New Spain again became preoccupied with other, more pressing problems so that for several more decades there was another period of neglect.

The groundwork, however, had been firmly established by Kino, so that when circumstances permitted, the Spaniards were able to operate from bases in Baja California, Sonora and Arizona. The drive for permanent settlements in California was hastened in the 1760's owing to an extraordinary confluence of circumstances. For one thing, the new King of Spain, Charles III, crowned in 1759, was an intelligent, enlightened monarch quite unlike his incompetent predecessor. Secondly, the Seven Years' War (1759–1763) had changed the political face of North America, especially in that England, Spain's long-time rival, had pushed the French off the continent, and Louisiana had become Spanish territory. The French threat was ended, but the incipient menace of an England growing ever more powerful alarmed Spain. Furthermore Russia loomed on the horizon as a potential threat; the Big Bear had colonized in Alaska and claimed territory much further south.

In 1765 Charles III appointed the capable and energetic José de Galvez as Visitador-General (a special, temporary post with powers superseding those of the permanently appointed Viceroy); this procedure afforded the Spanish monarch an additional measure of personal control over the viceregal representative situated months away from New Spain. Galvez threw himself into the herculean task of resolving the many problems that troubled New Spain. High on the order of his priorities was to strengthen New Spain's frontier outposts, and he was particularly concerned with settling California.

The Visitador authorized a combined sea and land expedition. The land forces, the most important part of the combined plan, under the civil and military command of Don Gaspar de Portolá, set out from the frontier post of Velicatá in Baja California in March of 1769. Portolá, a Creole born and bred on the frontier, was an experienced soldier, and possessed the resourcefulness and courage of a leader.

An advance party, led by Fernando Rivera y Moncada, after seven weeks of marching reached San Diego where the men of the city reinforced the small group that reached the port by sea. Two months later they were joined by the main group led by Portolá. The first major step in settling California had been accomplished, but it was obvious that the surviving half of the three hundred men who had started out from Velicatá had much to do.

Accompanying the expedition were a number of friars of the Franciscan order which had replaced the Jesuit missionaries as the advance agents of the Church and Crown. The Jesuits had been ousted in 1767 after more than two hundred years of missionary work throughout the Spanish colonies in the New World. The order which had become a huge international organization with valuable properties located all over the world, had aroused the jealousy of other

Father Junípero Serra, the eighteenth century
Franciscan explorer, mission-builder and friend
of the Indians.

regular orders, and was considered too powerful by the heads of state in western Europe. In fact, their power was so threatening that in 1759 the Jesuits were expelled from the Catholic Portuguese empire; in 1764 His Catholic Majesty, Louis XIV, ordered their expulsion from all French territory; and in 1767 Louis' Bourbon cousin, Charles III, ordered the expulsion of the order from all Spanish lands. Finally, in 1775 the Pope suppressed the Society of Jesus and it was not until 1814 that it was reestablished.

The missions and other outposts that had been organized by Father Kino and many other Jesuits in Baja California and in Pimería Alta were then turned over to the Franciscan order. Therefore, when Portolá commenced his operations, he was accompanied by Franciscan fathers who had been functioning in the area for about two years. One of the friars was Junípero Serra, an outstanding pioneer of early California history.

Serra has been described as "an enthusiastic, battling, almost quarrelsome, fearless, keen-witted, fervidly devout, unselfish, single-minded missionary" by the distinguished historian of California, Charles Edward Chapman. More than that, Serra was an excellent administrator and a scholar interested in the science of agriculture and in handicrafts. He was also a mystic with a penchant for suffering who yearned for a martyr's death.

While the march to San Diego had been relatively uneventful, the men were exhausted after having crossed several hundred miles of desert, climbed steep hills and descended innumerable barrancas. Despite their exhaustion, they were driven by Portolá to build a mission station, San Diego Alcalá, for Father Serra. Then Portolá, with a small group of hardy soldiers and another Franciscan friar, Juan Crespi, moved northward.

While searching for the Bay of Monterey that had been so effusively described by Vizcaíno two hundred years before, on November 1 they stumbled upon an even more magnificent natural harbor, so large that "not only all the navy of our most Catholic Majesty but those of all Europe could take shelter." That first description of San Francisco Bay was recorded in Father Crespi's meticulously kept diary. It is amazing that the many sea expeditions had not located San Francisco Bay thus discovered so accidentally by an overland group!

Apparently because Portolá lacked the necessary imagination, or because he had been ordered by Galvez to find and establish a port in Monterey, the Creole gave short shrift to his discovery of San Francisco Bay, and doggedly continued on his search for Monterey. For another month the haggard men searched fruitlessly for the bay which was not easily perceived from the pine covered hills surrounding it. On December 9, a discouraged and disappointed Portolá turned back. Despite their frontier expertise and the abundance of wild game, the men suffered from lack of food. During the last twelve days they consumed the tough meat of as many pack mules. Portolá wrote that "we shut our eyes and fell on to that scaly mule . . . like hungry lions" after having half roasted the meat "in a fire made in a hole in the ground."

From San Diego, Portolá organized a second expedition, a combined land and sea operation, to Monterey, which they reached on March 24, 1770. The bay was so naturally concealed by groves of trees that it was only by accident that Father Crespi and two soldiers who were walking along the beach toward the Carmel River "perceived that the bay was locked by points Año Nuevo and Piños, in such a manner that the great bay resembled a round lake like an O." Then they suddenly realized that this indeed was the port of Monterey which they had been seeking.

Having fulfilled his assignment, and not wanting to settle in the wilderness, Portolá returned to Mexico City where he reported his findings to the Viceroy and the Visitator.

During the following three years, five mission stations were built, including the famous San Gabriel just north of San Diego, and the San Luis Obispo mission on the central coast of California. Eventually twenty-one missions in all formed a chain of settlements along seven hundred miles of coast.

These distant outposts of the empire were doomed to isolation unless an overland route from Sonora could be opened. Such a road would guarantee continuity of supplies and regular communication, and encourage settlers from New Spain. Thus, explorations initiated by the Franciscan padre Francisco Garcés in the deserts of southern California were useful.

Garcés' exploits inspired a frontier captain in Sonora, Juan Bautista de Anza, to attempt a daring plan of exploration. However, such plans required the prior approval of the viceroy and that entailed the usual petitioning, consultations, and so on. Anza petitioned the viceroy in May, 1772. After consulting with the approving Father Serra, who happened to be in Mexico City, Viceroy Bucareli authorized the expedition in September of the following year. Then came a period of outfitting, recruiting and planning so that it was not until January of 1774 that Anza and Garcés set out from Sonora.

The expedition of twenty soldiers, many muleteers and servants, a pack train of supplies, sixty-five head of cattle and one hundred and fifty horses met with difficulties almost from the outset. An Apache raid resulted in the loss of some mules and horses, part of the price paid for following the hazardous trail known as Devil's Road to the junction of the Colorado and Gila rivers. Fortunately the Yuma Indians, whose agricultural skills were admired by the Spaniards, were friendly.

Then came weeks spent in crossing burning sands, followed by the difficult ascent of the San Jacinto mountains. They were rewarded, finally, by the sight of "some most beautiful valleys, very green and flower strewn; snowy mountains with live oaks and other trees native to cold lands. The waters, too, are divided, some running on this side of the Gulf, and others to the Philippine Islands." Obviously, while Anza was an intrepid explorer, he was not much of a geographer.

After two months the Anza and Garcés group reached the San Gabriel mission, whose occupants were pleasantly surprised that anyone could have come from Sonora. Anza rested and then set out to return to Sonora. He reached his destination taking almost five months and riding about twenty-two hundred miles to make the complete trip. Viceroy Bucareli showed his pleasure by promoting Anza to the rank of lieutenant colonel and designating him as head of a colonizing expedition.

This time, in addition to the usual complement of soldiers, approximately two hundred and forty colonists, more than half of them children, were to make the long trip. While Anza led one group following the trail he had previously blazed, Father Garcés and a smaller group successfully essayed another route over the Mojave Trail which led between desert and coast to San Gabriel. The historian Herbert Bolton comments that the Garcés feat was "one of the epic journeys of all North American history."

Anza's force reached San Gabriel after Garcés, then, following the viceroy's orders, he marched northward. At the Bay of San Francisco, Anza arranged for the building of two missions and a *presidio* (garrison) and then left for Sonora. At the very time that Anza was completing his historic journey, unsurpassed in the annals of North American exploration and colonial migration, the founding fathers of the Anglo-American colonies were discussing the Declaration of Independence.

For a while a small, but steady stream of settlers departed from New Spain to colonize California. However the path so heroically opened by Anza and Garcés found very limited use after 1781 when the Yuma Indians, no longer so friendly, attacked two missions near the Colo-

Restoration of one of the earliest Spanish missions at a Zuñi pueblo.

rado–Gila junction and killed many Spaniards, including Father Garcés and Fernando Rivera y Moncada, the explorer and former governor of California. After the Yuma uprising, California was left pretty much on its own, to remain a distant, almost isolated outpost of the New Spain colony, which supplied governors and little else. The missions and settlements were strung out along hundreds of miles of the coast. The interior, the major part of what is now known as California, was untouched.

Texas  For more than a hundred years after the conquest of Mexico, the Spaniards paid little attention to Texas. The El Paso district, a small expanse southeast of New Mexico, was settled about the same time as New Mexico. A few Franciscan missionaries had made feeble attempts to penetrate the vast territory and had come in contact with the Tejas (hence, Texas) and the Jumano Indians between 1650 and 1683. However, it was not until another European power, France, loomed on the horizon that New Spain bestirred itself.

In the competition for empire, France had been a bold contender in the New World, with Canada on the North American continent and many islands in the Caribbean. The colonists in Quebec, in their thirst for furs, had penetrated westward to the Great Lakes. La Salle had descended the Mississippi River to its mouth in the very year that New Spain was occupied with putting down the revolt of the Pueblo Indians. Although Spain claimed the Mississippi and its valley by virtue of De Soto's earlier explorations, nothing had been done in the way of assuming control of this area. Thus René Robert Cavalier, Sieur de la Salle, France's greatest explorer in the New World, disregarded Spanish pretensions and claimed the immense area—later to become almost two-thirds of the continental United States—for Louis XIV, after whom the territory was named Louisiana.

The French manner of dealing with the Indians was considerably different from that of the Spaniards. The latter offered salvation and enslavement; whereas the French offered brandy, guns and knives. The Spaniards forced the Indians to adopt Spanish clothing, language, and customs, and compelled nomadic tribes to adopt a sedentary existence. The French lived with the Indians, learned and adopted their ways, wandered with them, and sought only the advantages of the fur trade. The French methods generally were successful; one of the exceptions occurred in East Texas where attempts to found a permanent settlement met with disaster.

However the very presence of the French alarmed the Spaniards. In 1689 they dispatched Alonso de León, then governor of Coahuila, and Father Damián Massanet, a Franciscan missionary, along with 110 soldiers. They discovered the ruins of the French fort in East Texas, the occupants of which had been massacred by Indians.

The following year León led a larger force of soldiers and priests back to Texas to establish the first Spanish mission and military post in eastern Texas. Like its French predecessor, the Spanish mission had a short life. An epidemic took the lives of many Indians and Spaniards, livestock was lost and stolen, and finally the Indians rebelled against the missionaries' demand that they live in organized communities. The disheartened Spaniards abandoned the mission after a few months. Spain joined France in ignoring eastern Texas.

In 1699 three missions were built near the banks of the Rio Grande in response to rumors that the French were settling in Louisiana. Still there were no settlements until 1731 when the first civil authority was established in Texas, at

Fort St. John the Baptist—one of the three missions. During the next twenty years there was a minimum of expansion, mostly along or near the banks of the Rio Grande. Interest in Texas waned once again when France ceded Louisiana to Spain in 1762.

Throughout the eighteenth century the settlements in the border regions developed slowly and, generally, uneventfully. Of course there was continuous warfare with Indians, but the colonists learned to accept that as part of a way of life. Ranching and farming prospered, but slowly. Trade grew, but not exceptionally. There was some mining, but nothing to compare with the rich mines of Mexico. The whole area simply did not prove attractive enough for significant numbers of Mexicans. The borderlands lacked the mineral wealth and organized civilizations that characterized the central valley of Mexico. The northern provinces did not have large numbers of Indians which the Spaniards needed, and which they had in central Mexico, to work on the land and in the mines. The borderlands remained distant outposts of the empire on the eve of Mexico's independence.

> Slavery and all caste distinc-
> tions are abolished; all
> citizens are to be known simply
> as Americans.
> José María Morelos

## CHAPTER IV

# New Spain Becomes Mexico

IN 1821 THE RESIDENTS OF NEW SPAIN AND THE SOUTH-west were transformed very unmagically from being Spaniards to Mexicans.

True, they may have been called "Mexicans" before, but that term defined them as residents of a particular area, a geographic identification of that very large group of Spanish colonists. By way of comparison, one might note that the population of the thirteen Anglo-American colonies was predominantly English; and, if before independence they were called "Americans" it was by way of distinguishing them from Englishmen in other parts of the British empire.

To continue the comparison, one might note among the "Americans" that there was further self-imposed classification whereby individuals were identified by the colony in which they lived: Virginians, Pennsylvanians, and so forth. The Spanish-speaking inhabitants of the Southwest, before 1821, called themselves Californios, New Mexicans, Texans. And because of their relative isolation from the center of affairs in New Spain, that classification was often more

Father Miguel Hidalgo, leader of the Mexican war
of independence and father of his country.

meaningful than the name "Spaniard" or "Mexican." Generally, it was the officials appointed by the viceroy who identified with Mexico City or even distant Madrid.

When the great war of independence began in 1810 in New Spain, the peoples of the borderlands were more or less indifferent, most of the time playing a passive role. Nevertheless, the achievement of independence had far-reaching effects upon them, and the struggle against Spain is a very important part of the history and heritage of the Mexican-American today. It is a complex story spanning the years from 1808 to 1821.

The event which sparked the revolutions in the Spanish colonies overseas was the invasion of Spain in 1808 by Napoleon, who placed his brother, Joseph, upon the throne. This aroused the bitter opposition of Spaniards who increased their resistance against the French; guerrilla warfare made French occupation a nightmare. The French invasion fanned the embers of independence in the New World where Creoles, long resentful of Spanish domination, took advantage of the turmoil in Spain.

In New Spain, the first of several revolutionary leaders to undertake the struggle for independence was the obscure village priest, Father Miguel Hidalgo y Costilla. On September 16, 1810, in the square of the tiny village of Dolores, Hidalgo addressed thousands of assembled Indians, urging them to rebel against the Spaniards. At the conclusion of his harangue, Hidalgo shouted: "Long live America! Long live religion! Down with bad government!", the famous *Grito de Dolores* (the Cry of Dolores). The memorable scene is relived every September 16 in the Zócalo—the immense square in Mexico City, when the President thus concludes the ceremonies celebrating Independence Day.

To the slogans presented by Hidalgo, the enthusiastic

Indians added the cry, "Death to the *gachupines!*" (a term of derision applied by the native born to the officials, and their sycophants, who came directly from Spain).

The Indian supporters of Hidalgo's movement adopted a religious symbol, the Virgin of Guadalupe, long the patroness of New Spain. In 1531, a poor Indian convert, Juan Diego, claimed to have seen the Virgin on a small hill near Tlalteloco. The reigning Bishop, after checking the story, attested to the genuineness of the Indian's story. A statue of a dark-skinned Virgin was erected and the site consecrated. In 1754, the Pope declared the Virgin of Guadalupe the Patroness and Protectress of New Spain. Now, in 1810, the Indians called upon her to be the patroness and protectress of the Revolution. The Shrine of the Virgin of Guadalupe remains the holiest in Mexico, and as recently as 1945 she was awarded the additional honor of being named Queen of Wisdom of the Americas. Brown replicas of the statue are found in the homes of many Mexican-Americans today. A statue of Our Lady of Guadalupe keeps watch in the office of César Chávez, the leader of the farm workers. To the poor Mexican-Americans, many of whom are part Indian, the Virgin is, quite naturally, brown. Many say she was an Indian, and that perhaps, God is brown.

The revolt in New Spain began as a popular uprising of masses of Indians, inspired by a few Creoles like Hidalgo. This popular movement was directed against the centuries-long oppression, misery and humiliation that the masses of New Spain had endured. Hidalgo, also, was intent on the redress of the many grievances of the Indians and *mestizos,* the overwhelming majority of the population. Among the social reforms he hoped to realize was the abolition of Negro slavery, one of the first attempts in the Western Hemisphere to end that infamous institution. He tried to abolish the tribute that Indians had to pay, and supported the idea that Indian land should be cultivated by Indians for their own benefit, but these, and the other humanitarian reforms he attempted to institute, were not realized. The poorly equipped army of undisciplined Indians was defeated by royalist forces and Hidalgo was forced to flee.

His escape route brought him to Texas, where his cause was betrayed by a Colonel Ignacio Elizondo, who had switched sides to give his support to the royalist commander, Manuel Zambrano. Zambrano had put down a feeble insurgent movement in Texas and had declared himself ruler of Texas and the neighboring province of Coahuila. The escaping Hidalgo and some of his co-conspirators were captured in an ambush at Baján set by the Mexican Benedict Arnold, Elizondo. Hidalgo was executed, but the cause that the Father of Mexican Independence had set in motion continued.

Leadership was picked up by another obscure village priest, Father José María Morelos, the curate of Carácuaro. Despite the fact that Hidalgo and his supporters had been excommunicated by the Bishop, Morelos decided to join the revolutionists. Hidalgo had appointed him a lieutenant, to conduct military operations in the south. After Hidalgo's execution in May, 1811, Morelos assumed the leadership of the revolutionary forces.

Like Hidalgo, Morelos was unselfishly dedicated to the Indians and to the need for social, economic and political reform. He, too, proclaimed the abolition of Indian tribute, slavery and the caste system. His denunciation of the caste system merits special notice. He contended that it was disparaging and hateful to make the distinctions of mulatto, Indian, mestizo, Creole, zambo and so on. All inhabitants, regardless of color or ethnic background, should be known as Americans. This forthright egalitarian approach was, for Morelos, true Christianity. It was certainly truly humanistic as well as far-sighted, anticipating by many decades the hopes of those individuals who favor a society in which men and women will be appreciated as individuals and not distinguished by any classification based on color of skin or ethnic composition.

Mixtures of different ethnic groups had progressed uninterruptedly from 1492 on. Spaniards, claiming purity of blood, had formed unions with Indians; the offspring was called a *mestizo*. Some unions with blacks produced mulattoes. Subsequently there was a bewildering variety of mixtures such as those of mestizos with Indians, with whites, with mulattoes, with blacks, and so forth. The Spanish officials, foolishly attempting to classify the most common mixtures, listed more than twenty.

The absurdity is pointed up in many ways. In the United States, if one's ancestors three or four or more generations earlier were Mexican, then one is considered to be a Mexican-American the same as someone who has migrated here only a few years ago from Mexico. A black person, who might have three white grandparents is still considered black. The great black poet, Langston Hughes, caustically commented that Negro blood must be truly powerful, because white blood did not count. In the Spanish colonies, on the other hand, anyone who could prove that one of his ancestors was a white Spaniard, legally could purchase a document certifying him, or her, as white. In effect the Spaniards were saying that Negro or Indian blood was unimportant because white blood was so powerful!

That Morelos as long ago as 1813 was able to see through the hypocrisy of such classifications is a tribute to his far-sighted humanism. This modest, gentle man, because of his

Father José María Morelos, the Mexican patriot who
continued the struggle for independence after
Hidalgo was executed.

avowed dedication to the brotherhood of man, earned the hatred of all the conservative elements in New Spain.

Morelos practiced what he preached. His closest associates were Hermenegildo Galeana, grandson of an English buccaneer who had settled in Mexico; Nicolás Bravo and his four brothers, wealthy Creoles; Vicente Guerrero, a poor mestizo peasant; Mariano Matamoros, a poor mestizo priest; Guadalupe Victoria, a mestizo; Peter Ellis Bean, an American soldier of fortune who had been captured during a filibustering expedition in Texas in 1800, and who escaped from the Spaniards in 1810 to join Morelos; and Valerio Trujano, a mulatto.

Morelos' basic gentleness did not prevent him from being a most capable military commander who led his armies in many victories against the royalists. His military exploits came to an end dramatically in 1815 when he allowed himself to be captured in order to save the leaders of the Congress.

The "Servant of the Nation" was tried by the officers of the Inquisition as well as by those of the royalist government. The Inquisitors found him guilty on twenty six charges and declared him "a heretic, apostate of the holy faith, an atheist, materialist, deist, libertine, implacable enemy of Christianity and the state, a vile seducer, hypocrite and traitor." The royalist government, after holding a separate three-day trial, condemned Morelos as a traitor. The humble priest was publicly defrocked, bound, blindfolded, and compelled to kneel to receive two volleys in the back.

A century later, President Lázaro Cárdenas (1934–1940) ordered the erection of a gigantic statue of Morelos atop the peak of the island of Janitzio in Lake Pátzcuaro where one of Mexico's most illustrious heroes now stands majestic, silent vigil.

Hidalgo and Morelos were not the only priests who sided with the cause of independence. Those who did were in every instance priests at the bottom of the church hierarchy. The official position of the Church and the attitude of the members of the upper echelons of the clergy were consistently conservative, if not reactionary. The Hidalgos were excommunicated. The blessings of the Church, and its financial support, went to the royalists.

The economic resources of the Church were tremendous. Lucas Alamán, conservative and devout Catholic, statesman and eminent historian, estimated that the total property of the clergy "certainly was not less than half of the total value of the real estate of the country," and protested that the Church had become economically too powerful for its own good. In view of its great economic power and, in general, its conservative stance throughout the colonial period, it is not surprising that Church authorities were unalterably opposed to social reforms proposed by Fathers Hidalgo and Morelos. Although they were both fervent and loyal Catholics, the opposition of the Church stemmed from social, economic and political disagreements, not religious motives or religious differences.

With Hidalgo and Morelos dead, the movement for independence not only lost its most inspiring leaders, but the character of the struggle changed. From the military point of view, the struggles that continued were guerrilla actions with no one chieftain representing all the revolutionary forces. There was no longer a leadership pledged to racial equality and to the abolition of slavery which would fight against clerical and military privileges or for restoration of land to the Indians.

The independence movement took a strange twist as a consequence of events in Spain. In the home country, insurgents fighting against Napoleon had adopted a progressive constitution which the arch-conservative elements in New Spain found intolerable. With Napoleon safely out of the way, liberal elements in Spain had set up a constitutional monarchy. The conservatives in New Spain who had opposed independence now favored it. A devious plot enabled them to seize the leadership of the movement to guarantee conservative control of an independent nation. What had started out as movement for generous social and economic reform was transformed into a movement for independence that would guarantee the preservation of the old ways. When independence did come in September of 1821, New Spain, now Mexico, would be ruled by a combination of conservative Creoles and Church leaders instead of by Spaniards and Church leaders. The misery of the ruled remained about the same, if not worse.

During the eleven years of fighting for independence, most of the inhabitants of the frontier provinces remained isolated and uninvolved. For the first years there were some sparks of rebellion in Texas, but royalist forces handily suppressed any open support for the revolutionists. When independence did come it was no cause for special rejoicing in the Southwest where people were more concerned with the normal pursuits of living. Instead of being provinces of New Spain, a colony of Spain, they were now provinces of Mexico. Instead of being ruled indirectly from Mexico City, the provinces were ruled directly from that great metropolis. Their relative isolation remained almost the same.

In September of 1821, the leader of the army of independence, Agustín Iturbide, a former royalist commander who had opportunely switched sides, became the provisional head of the new government. In May, 1822 he proclaimed himself Emperor Agustín I. The news reached Monterey, California in September; the Spanish flag was lowered and replaced by the new imperial banner of Mexico. In November of 1823, Agustín I was overthrown in a bloodless revolution and a republic was proclaimed. Almost two years later, California and the other provinces acknowledged the new change. Province of New Spain, province of the Empire of Mexico, province of the Republic of Mexico. The changes did not seem to matter. They certainly were of no consequence to the Indians.

The Church emerged from the War of Independence even more powerful than before. During the fighting the Church gained new lands and new mortgages. Whereas previously the Spanish monarchy had exerted some control over the Church, now the Church in Mexico became entirely independent, with great influence on the government.

The chief partner of the Church in dominating political affairs was the army. The generals, like the clergy, became a power independent of the government.

Democracy was conspicuous by its absence. For several decades Mexico was to be ruled by a succession of incompetent tyrants who came in and out of power according to the whims of some general, supported by the Church.

The Republic was divided into nineteen states and four territories; the area in the Southwest was part of the four territories.

During the twenty-five-year period between gaining independence and war with the United States, Mexico suffered the turbulence of tyrants, corruption and increasing banditry. In the northern territories, excepting Texas, life was relatively calm, although far from idyllic, for most of the inhabitants.

In Mexico, the general who appears and disappears numerous times was Antonio López de Santa Anna. He held office no less than eleven times. He was a semi-perpetual dictator who wielded power even when not in office, for he made and unmade presidents.

The political situation bordered on anarchy. In each state, powerful *caudillos,* leaders who personally controlled local armies, exercised virtual autonomy, lending or withdrawing their support to the central government as it suited their personal ambitions. Periodically some *caudillo* would issue a *pronunciamento,* a *Plan* would be announced, and a change of government leaders would ensue.

The *hacendados* grew richer and many more Indians and *mestizos* became bound by peonage. The Church grew richer and more powerful, despite some attempts by liberals to introduce reforms.

In the territories there were no spectacular developments. Each area developed in relative isolation from the others and had minimum contact with the metropolitan center of the republic. One significant common characteristic was the inherent provincialism of the society.

In California, the twenty-one Franciscan missions dominated not only religious life but also economic life in the territory until 1836. In that year, the liberals in Mexico succeeded in achieving a basic reform which they had hoped to institute in all Mexico. Their intention was to limit the economic power of the Church by taking over most of its income-producing properties. They initiated the reform in California, but were prevented from carrying it out elsewhere. The missions in California were secularized; all the income-producing properties were taken over by the government and sold or leased to private individuals.

Great herds of livestock, including some 400,000 head of cattle, 60,000 horses, 300,000 sheep, goats and swine, as well as millions of acres of land were transferred to private owners. Lands which produced annually tens of thousands of bushels of wheat, maize, beans and other farm produce came under private ownership. Between 15,000 to 30,000 Indians were released, some to return to the wilderness, some to work for private rancheros and hacendados instead of for the Franciscan friars. The proceeds and apparatus of foreign trade, previously monopolized by the missions, were turned over to private merchants. The missions' production of wine, brandy, soap, leather, hides, wool, cotton, hemp, linen, tobacco, salt and caustic soda (which gives some measure of the commercial activities of the church) likewise changed hands.

The Church in California after 1836 no longer dominated the economic life of the area. In its place rich hacendados, ranchers and merchants became the ruling class. In just a few years about eight million prime acres were divided among eight hundred hacendados and rancheros. By 1846, forty-six of them were so extremely rich that they ruled California.

After 1836 the rambling, spacious and luxurious homes built by wealthy people contrasted sharply with their simple adobe, earthen-floored houses of the past. The rich styled themselves as *gente de razón,* or people of reason, but that should not be construed to mean that they were well educated or given to cultural and intellectual pursuits. Most of them were illiterate, unable even to write their names. There were no schools in California except the mission-operated schools for religious indoctrination. There were no newspapers, libraries, theatres, museums or any other such cultural resources.

Entertainment, especially at fiestas celebrating a religious holy day or at the end of one of the big cattle roundups, consisted of nights and days of dancing, guitar playing, *cor-*

*rido* (Mexican-style ballad) singing and barbecues at which liberal quantities of food and wine were made available for everyone. The men were fond of horse-racing, cock-fighting, bear and bull-baiting, and addicted to gambling. They lived a vigorous outdoor life, were free from the tensions of contemporary society, and were genuinely hospitable. Life was gracious, if simple. For the poor, whether white, *mestizo* or Indian, life was simple, but hardly gracious.

The cattle industry became the single most important enterprise, and the entire economy depended on it. However, just as in Mexico, where ranching had its origins, cattle were not raised primarily for beef but for hides and tallow. There was more than enough meat for all, but none for export. There were several reasons for this: lack of a system of transportation, no refrigeration to preserve the meat; and, there were no large markets or large centers of population near enough to warrant driving large herds of cattle or sheep. Railroads, refrigeration, large centers of population did not come into existence for several decades.

The hides, used for a variety of purposes, could be more easily transported. Tallow, fat which was used in cooking and grease obtained for the manufacture of soap and candles, was the other principal product. Tallow and hides were the principal exports. Cattle, therefore, was the chief source of wealth, trade, food and occupation.

Although it is beginning to undergo radical changes now in the urban areas, the close-knit family, including grandparents, parents, children, uncles and aunts, cousins and in-laws, is a continuation of an institution that is profoundly Mexican. It is a way of life scarcely disturbed in the course of several hundred years and continues throughout the southwest among Spanish-speaking inhabitants. *La familia,* is one of the surest signs of *mexicanidad,* or "Mexican-ness."

(The extended family is a social feature common to Latin Americans.)

However, foreigners eventually penetrated into this provincial community. French, English, Germans and Americans, mostly traders, visited the shores of California. American fur trappers and traders made their way overland. Most were highly critical of the Californio way of life. A few were enamoured of it, stayed on, married into the most respectable families, adopted the language and the customs, and became Californios themselves. The change was definitely true for their descendants. That was not typical, for from the first contacts the Anglo-Americans, imbued with supremacist ideas and used to completely different customs, viewed the Californios with contempt, and acted accordingly.

The New Mexican territory, which included Arizona, developed along paths at once similar to and quite different from, California. In 1810 as in California, Spanish-Mexican customs and traditions still prevailed among the 35,000 Spanish-speaking inhabitants. There were some 102 settlements, only three of which were large enough to be called towns—Santa Fe, Santa Cruz de la Cañada and Albuquerque.

Each of the smaller settlements were usually dominated by a single large family clan wresting a living from the semiarid land through cooperative farming or raising small herds of sheep on communal land bordering the village. It is this communal type of land ownership, modelled somewhat on the Aztec *calpulli,* of which some Hispanos of New Mexico are now dreaming. The dreams are being capitalized on by militant leaders, like Tijerina. There have been some attempts even to establish agricultural cooperatives reminiscent of the old communal operations.

The *rico,* or rich man, of New Mexico was the *patrón,*

patriarchal head of a self-sufficient community in which he wielded as much power as his California counterpart. Sheep raising was the major industry, although there was considerable cattle ranching and farming. The labor system was peonage, the system of debt slavery which kept the servant bound to the patrón for his lifetime. The ricos claimed pure Mexican, or Spanish, ancestry. Some traced their lineage to Oñate, Vargas, Cortés, or other illustrious names. Since the records had been destroyed during the Indian uprising of 1680, definite proof was lacking although some undoubtedly were genuine. The claim to "pure" Spanish blood was probably spurious; the estimate of historians is that about eighty per cent of the Spanish-speaking people were *mestizo*.

Twenty-six Pueblo Indian communities with about 10,000 inhabitants were scattered north and south of Santa Fe. The teachings of the Franciscan fathers had little lasting influence, nor had there been any considerable effects of Spanish culture among the Pueblos. Agriculture was their chief occupation, and they continued to employ ancient Indian methods of irrigation. Elsewhere, the Apaches remained aloof and unconquered, the implacable foe of the foreigner, a constant threat to isolated smaller communities, raiding trade caravans, restricting Mexican settlements mainly to a long, narrow corridor along the Rio Grande. Other nomadic tribes, the Utes, Navajos and sometimes the Comanches, also plagued the settlers with raids. It was not always a case of New Mexicans defending themselves against attack; often they initiated raids, one object of which was to capture Indians to be used as domestic servants.

The presence of hostile Indians, and other factors such as the bleak winters, the semiarid condition of much of the settled areas, an inefficient, corrupt and unstable government in distant Mexico City, and the isolation from major cultural centers combined to make life in New Mexico rather grim when compared with life on the ranches in California. Californians had the additional advantage of coming into contact with people of many nations whose ships occasionally touched at California's spacious harbors. However, in the provincial capital of Santa Fe, as well as in the very large haciendas, there were moments of gaiety, especially on the many religious holidays.

On such occasions the landed gentry wore their very best. The *hidalgo*,* a gentleman from a rich family, wore a flat-topped, black sombrero equipped with chin strap, woolen pantaloons, leather leggings, an ornate leather jacket, hand-made finely tooled leather boots, and a delicately woven, colorful serape. The mounts of the hidalgos were small, wiry horses most likely descended from Arabian stock. Saddles were expensive and beautiful examples of the craftsmanship of leather and silver workers. The leather was hand-tooled, ornamented with silver; bridles were ornate and equipped with vicious bits to hold the capricious mustangs in check and to enable the rider to put his mount through intricate maneuvers.

Despite the comparatively luxurious way of life of wealthy hidalgos who could afford to import some expensive goods, trade was minimal. The self-sufficient economic existence of agricultural communities was more conducive to subsistence living rather than to commercial development. Such trade as was conducted was made difficult by the long routes constantly under threat of Indian attack. When the Anglo-American trader started to move in after Mexico became independent, changes were gradually introduced, especially in the northernmost regions of the territory.

First came the trappers—French and Anglo-Americans

---

* *hidalgo*—derived from *hijo de algo,* son of something. Originally the lowest rank of nobility in Spain. Many dubious claims to the title were made by "sons of something" in the New World.

from Missouri—free and independent of the big fur companies. In Taos, and subsequently in Santa Fe, enterprising American merchants set up permanent trading posts and began to develop a brisk trade. Most of the trappers and traders came and departed. By 1846, only 150 merchants had settled permanently and many of them had intermarried with Mexican families. Mexicans also began to find that merchandising was a profitable venture; by 1840 one of the best "stores" in Santa Fe was owned and operated by Don Juan Sena.

The stimulus of trade opened up new markets for arts and crafts in which New Mexicans excelled. Silver craftsmen produced silverware for the table and household ornaments. Cabinetmakers turned out exquisite pieces of furniture like cupboards, chests and chairs with loving care; the art of the woodcarver was seen on doors, lintels, corbels and posts. Jewelers working with silver and gold designed beautiful lacelike pieces of filigree. Needleworkers and weavers, spinners and dyers produced lovely cloths in cotton and in wool. In all these art forms one notes the influence of Indian design and craftsmanship.

The Arizona portion of the New Mexican territory was isolated more than its neighbors to the east or west. There was no single settlement of importance, no missions that could approach the prosperity of those in California or in New Mexico, no great estates or haciendas that had any permanence. By 1846 there were perhaps two thousand Mexicans, almost all very poor, living in constant dread of the Apaches. Arizona did not fit into the plans of either colonial New Spain or of independent Mexico.

Texas was the least developed and the least settled of the territories, except for Arizona. Most attempts to colonize the area were in response to foreign threats. The presence of numerous hostile Indians and the savage character of the territory did not entice settlers from New Spain. During the last half of the eighteenth century settlements did grow along the Rio Grande; and after Mexican independence was achieved, settlers were encouraged, with the aid of large land grants, to settle in the area between the Rio Grande and the Nueces rivers. Yet by 1836 there were still no more than 5,000 Mexicans in Texas. The largest settlement was that of San Antonio with about 2,000; La Bahia, later to be called Goliad, was next with about 1,400; and at Nacogdoches there were no more than 500.

The big landowners, mostly *mestizos,* lived in a style similar to the early Californios. The peóns, mostly Indian, lived a debt-ridden, miserable existence. In sharp contrast to the luxurious ranch homes of their patróns, the peóns lived in one-room, thatched-roofed, dirt-floor hovels called *jacales.* The wealthy Tejanos, more than their Californian and New Mexican peers, followed Mexican customs and traditions and their children were sent to private and parochial schools in Mexico. The physical proximity to Mexico probably accounted for the closer ties.

The border regions were no longer distant outposts of empire. On the eve of their conquest by the United States they had become slightly more developed outposts—of a republic, torn with internal dissension and incompetent government.

> The right of conquest has no
> foundation other than the right
> of the strongest.
> Jean Jacques Rousseau

## CHAPTER V

# Conquest of the Southwest by the Americans

THE AMERICAN SOUTHWEST HAD GONE THROUGH SEVERAL periods of diverse development before its conquest by the United States. At first, the inhabitants had been Indians of different tribes at varying stages of social development who had occupied the land for some twenty thousand years. The Indians were conquered by Spaniards and Creoles. That period of conquest and settlement took place over a period of about 250 years.

The total population—Indian, Spanish, Creole, black, and the many mixtures—never exceeded 150,000. Settlements were small islands of humanity dispersed over wide expanses, most of which remained wilderness and uninhabited deserts. When in 1821 New Spain achieved independence and became Mexico, the Mexicans in the borderlands were just that: inhabitants of territory far from the center of Mexican life who were left pretty much alone to conduct their own affairs.

Before the Mexicans of the Southwest became Mexican-Americans by virtue of the conquest by the United States, they had made a number of significant contributions—many of which had lasting effects.

Most obvious was the language, Spanish—the Mexican variety now interlaced with terms that were from the New World. This included not just the spoken language, but also the literature, including the great classics of the Golden Age of Spain as well as the lesser contributions of New Spain and Mexico. The language left an indelible stamp upon the whole area in that literally *thousands* of place names are Spanish: buildings, churches, missions, streets, towns, cities, counties, states, mountains, valleys, rivers. The names of hundreds of objects are Spanish: vegetables, fruits, herbs, flowers, trees, plants, animals, food. In addition hundreds of Spanish words have been Anglicized, such as: banana, barbecue, cockroach, canary, canoe, cannibal, cigar, cocoa, filibuster, hammock, Negro, stampede.

Cattle ranching—the entire institution in all its aspects—was Mexican in origin and was well developed before the first permanent English settlement in Jamestown in 1607. Americans brought up on American fiction, Hollywood movies and television are reasonably familiar with many aspects of cattle ranching which they view as being typically American. In particular, Texas-style ranching with the Texan cowboy, ten-gallon hat and all, are portrayed in the "westerns" as being inherently Texan. Nothing could be further from the truth.

The word "cowboy," or better, cowman, a translation from the Mexican *vaquero,* came into use in Texas in 1836. The first cattle were driven into Texas by Mexicans as early as 1690, although it was 1721 before large numbers of livestock were brought there. The first migrant Americans to Texas came about one century later and found a well-developed cattle industry which, with minor modifications, they adopted as their own. The new Texans, that is to say, the Americans, borrowed methods, equipment, and language from their Mexican predecessors.

The horned saddle, borrowed from the Moors by the Spaniards long before, was a specially adapted piece of equipment essential for cattle raising. The *vaquero* made his saddle usually from some soft wood such as the giant prickly pear; and the large silver horn served a number of practical uses, in particular when roping cattle or horses. *Dale vuelta* meant twisting a rope about the saddle horn; the Americans called it simply "dolly."

The rope employed by the *vaquero* was made of horse-hair, or *mecate*. It was called a *reata,* and used in lassoing; *la reata* became lariat, *lazo* became lasso. Equipment like the bridle, bit, spur, cinch, halter, stirrup tips, feedbag for the horse, all were adaptations from the Mexican. The Mexicans were using *chaparejos* as early as the 17th century. These leather leggings provided protection against the rough hide of the horse as well as against the spines of cactus, *mezquite* and other brush; the American cowboy borrowed them and called them "chaps." *Barboquejo* was the chin-strap for the *sombrero galoneado* which somehow was mistranslated as "ten-gallon hat." Many of the words of modern cattle ranching are still Spanish: rodeo, corrida, remuda, burro, corral, loco.

The *jinete* was the Mexican professional horsebreaker, a special craft which became part of the Texan technique. The practice of having a *remuda,* or group of horses to be used in relay to guarantee fresh mounts throughout the long day, is Mexican. The Americans learned the art of branding from the Mexicans. (And to give credit where it is due, the Mexicans had borrowed the idea from the Spaniards who had borrowed it from the Moors!) The first brand used in Mexico was that employed by Cortés, three Christian crosses; the time—about three hundred years before the establishment of Texas as a republic.

Since the cattle grazed on open range, the livestock of several cattle barons intermingled. The *rodeo,* or general roundup, was invented as early as the 1550's in order to facilitate the sorting out of the herds. Sometimes these rodeos entailed hundreds of horsemen, who, fanning out in a great circle, would drive the cattle toward a center. Officials, *jueces del campo* (field judges) held court under the open sky. The *vaqueros* would prod the cattle with long iron-tipped poles, separating the herds by recognizable brands. The judges equitably resolved all disputes arising over unbranded strays and calves, dividing them up among the stockmen and including a share of the unbranded animals to be turned over to the King's representatives. As early as the late sixteenth century, there were great roundups in the northern provinces of New Spain where there were more than three hundred horsemen driving hundreds of thousands of head of cattle; some owners had as many as 150,000 head, and 20,000 was considered an insignificant number. This custom, with minor adaptations, was employed throughout the American Southwest; impartial "cattle judges" employed by the stockmen settled all conflicting claims.

A knowledge of the ethnic composition of the early *vaqueros* is both revealing and relevant. Almost from the very beginning, before the middle of the sixteenth century, the *vaquero,* being a hired hand, was recruited from Spaniards occupying the bottom of the social scale. Spaniards who came to the New World for God, Gold and Glory did not expect to have to do manual labor. In time, many of the *vaqueros* were *mestizos* (the product of the union between

European and Indian), Indians, Blacks, mulattoes and *zambos* (the result of union between Black and Indian). Blacks had been forcibly dragged out of their African homelands to become slaves in the island colonies of the Spaniards. In Cuba, where cattle ranching was developed early, it was found that African Blacks, having had prior experience with livestock, could be employed most efficiently and profitably taking care of cattle, sheep, horses, hogs, mules, and oxen. Many of these Blacks, and mulattoes, were brought to New Spain. On the islands, black slaves worked on sugar, coffee, indigo, rice and tobacco plantations as well as serving as livestock specialists. In New Spain, it was the Indian and *mestizo* who were employed generally as unskilled labor on plantations; Blacks and mulattoes were employed almost exclusively in the more skilled occupations such as those needed in cattle raising. Long before African Blacks were brought to the Anglo-American colonies, they were functioning as *vaqueros* and at other skilled trades in New Spain. It is only in recent years that scholars have brought to light that there were Negro cowboys (and bandits, explorers, Indian fighters, army scouts) in Texas just before the American Civil War. However, the record must be further corrected, for it is known that there were Negro-Mexican—cowboys in the American Southwest in the early seventeenth century!

Hollywood "westerns" inform us that Texas cowboys often would freelance, wandering from ranch to ranch and even crossing state boundaries in a restless search for adventure or perhaps just because they chose to be independent. It is most probable that this custom arose from an earlier tradition found in New Spain in the sixteenth century. Many *vaqueros*—white, black, *mestizo,* mulatto—preferred to lead a vagabond's life. A Spanish official wrote that these migratory workers "strike terror to the heart of the population;

calling themselves *vaqueros,* they ride about armed with *desjarretaderas,* or scythes; they collect in bands and no one dares withstand them." Another official commented: "They are agile and hardy. Their breed grows apace, and trouble may well be brewing, for so-and-so is employing 300 of these mounted brigands as cowboys, and most of them are equipped with breastplates, harquebuses, scythes, and other weapons." Sometimes they rustled cattle, sometimes they looted and pillaged. Nevertheless the cattle ranchers were compelled to avail themselves of the skilled services of these nomads, of whom it was said: "Their presence is an evil, but their absence is a much greater one."

The sheep industry, almost as important as cattle ranching, also developed early in New Spain. Sheep raising had long been a major enterprise in Spain. About 1,300 merino sheep, especially prized for their fine wool, were brought from North Africa to Andalusia. By 1500 there were flocks totaling more than 3,000,000 whose owners ranked among the most important and richest men in the realm. The verdant meadows and lush valleys of the New World were natural grazing lands for sheep. In the northern provinces of New Spain, great prosperous sheep ranches rivaled the cattle industry for economic importance. And, just as in the instance of the cattle industry, sheep raising in all its manifold aspects, was brought into the Southwest where Mexicans perfected the techniques that were to become known as American.

"Bur-ro, *Southwestern U.S.* 1. a pack donkey. 2. any donkey (t. Sp., der. *burrico,* small horse . . . )." The *American College Dictionary* makes it abundantly clear that the word, burro, is derived from the Spanish and that it was popular in the Southwest. Burros and mules were important beasts of burden used in transport and in mines in New Spain.

Traders carrying merchandise within Mexico and from Mexico to the border regions made extensive use of the reliable, patient, incredibly strong pack animals that could withstand the extremes of cold and heat, the rigors of mountains and deserts. Caravans of dozens of mules were not uncommon; sometimes there were trains of more than a hundred mules. The drovers, or muleteers, were highly skilled and trusted men in whose charge were put very valuable cargoes. Most of the early muleteers were *mestizos,* Blacks and mulattoes. The animals, the institution of mule trains, the techniques—all were subsequently adapted by American traders, miners, prospectors and the army of the United States. As in so many other instances, it was easy to forget the origins of the system.

The entire region had been explored and mapped. Towns and cities had been established. Excellent harbors were functioning on the California coast. Most of the Indians had been pacified or subdued. For the oncoming American pioneers a firm base had been laid for further exploitation. This was far different from the situations that had been previously encountered by American explorers and pioneers. Since colonial days, Anglo-American westward expansion had been into undeveloped forests and plains that had not been inhabited by anyone other than Indians.

The drama that was to unfold has as its prologue the gradual penetration of the Southwest by Anglo-Americans. The first scene of Act I is the movement for the secession of Texas.

In 1835 Texans began the movement that led to their secession from the Mexican Republic. In 1846 the war began between the United States and Mexico which ended in the latter's ignominious defeat and the cession to the U.S. of about half of all Mexican land. In a history of Mexican-

Americans the details of those two wars have no special relevance. However, of paramount interest are the circumstances which led Mexico to lose so vast an area, and the consequences to Mexican-American inhabitants. Debate over the merits of the Anglo-American versus the Mexican views are also immaterial in this work. Yet, it will be important to know the Mexican view, especially in order to understand the thinking of the Mexican-Americans of today about this part of their heritage.

Anglo-Americans had been coming into the Southwest for decades and few came to stay permanently. But their very presence was viewed with mixed feelings by the Mexicans. Those who became fully adapted, accepting Mexican customs and marrying into Mexican families, were in turn accepted by the Mexicans. Those who were transients and those who behaved in an arrogant, indifferent and even hostile manner to Mexican ways, were viewed with growing distaste and suspicion.

After the purchase of the Louisiana Territory from France in 1803, land-hungry settlers from the United States began to look covetously at Texas. In 1819, with the independence movement in New Spain seemingly defeated for the moment, royalist officials favorably considered encouraging Anglo-Americans to settle in Texas. The Spanish officials were prompted by hopes that the Anglo-Americans would act as a buffer in contending with the irreconcilable Indians; secondly, they anticipated receiving needed revenue from taxes.

A contract providing a large land grant, was given to Moses Austin, a Connecticut-born American. Austin was to bring to Texas three hundred families, each of which was to receive a land grant. Death intervened before Moses could carry out his plans and, on instructions from his father,

Stephen Austin continued the venture. By late 1821 he and some hardy pioneers began to settle on land bordering the Brazos River. But now Stephen Austin had to deal with a new government, for in September Mexico had achieved its independence.

The chaotic situation in Mexico prevented a quick resolution of the problem, so that it was not until February of 1823 that the new Mexican Congress issued a decree which granted to Austin and his colleagues what they had been so impatiently awaiting. The new decree gave legal sanction to what came to be known as the *empresario* system. In effect, the Mexican government would grant a very large piece of land to some enterprising American, like Stephen Austin, in return for bringing settlers to Texas. The lid of Pandora's box was thrown wide open.

The empresario was given considerable authority, including the administration of civil government in the colony, and command of the local militia, with the rank of lieutenant colonel. Each family head was to receive one *sitio,* a square league, of land suitable for grazing and one *labor* (a smaller portion) of tillage land, a total of 4,605 acres. Unmarried men were granted one quarter of a *sitio*.

The conditions for becoming such a colonist were simple. Each applicant had to offer evidence of good character, was required to swear an oath of allegiance to the Mexican government, and had to be a Catholic, or convert, before entering Texas. Many of the new settlers ignored or gave lip service to that last condition, thus violating from the outset their agreement with their hosts. This violation was a harbinger of others to come.

The Anglo-Americans brought with them a knowledge of, and experience with, some of the trappings of democracy. It was a philosophy hateful to the Mexican elite. The democratic spirit of the newcomers stood in direct opposition to the patriarchal, aristocratic outlook of the *ricos* and was bound to lead to conflict.

The democracy of the Anglo-Americans had at least one serious limitation; many of the settlers brought slaves with them. Although slavery was still legal, almost all of the Blacks in Mexico were free by the end of the wars for independence. The Congress of the new republic began to consider the abolition of slavery, thereby alarming the Anglo-Texans whose love of liberty did not extend to Blacks. In 1827 the government of Coahuila-Texas (these two areas had been combined to form one department) passed a law which freed children born to slaves; in one, or at the most two generations, slavery would have disappeared. For a period of six months additional slaves could be brought into Texas. Empresarios hastened to fulfill their contracts and Anglo-Americans, with their slaves, poured into the territory.

The empresario system was successful. Austin's experiment encouraged others to follow suit. Whereas the "white" population of Texas was a mere 5,000 in 1821 it approached 30,000 in just nine years. By 1835 all of Texas was divided up into grants with the Brazos River colony remaining the most important. Austin was recognized as the spokesman for all the new Texans.

The new Texans took an oath of allegiance, became Mexican by law but remained Anglo-American in practice. They violated laws with impunity and called upon their original homeland to aid them in moments of distress. There may have been compelling reasons for such behavior. It was a fact that the Mexican government was incompetent, corrupt, unstable. It was a fact that it was difficult to respect laws constantly undergoing change and without the pres-

ence, in Texas, of effective law-interpreting and law-enforc-
ing agencies. Reforms were very much needed, and demands for reforms would seem justifiable.

There is no evidence that most Anglo-Texans mounted a
serious struggle for reforms. On the other hand there *is* evidence that they took matters into their own hands, not in
the spirit of reform, but in the spirit of rebellion. The first
such major crisis arose in 1826 when Benjamin Edwards,
an empresario who had settled near Nacogdoches, initiated
an abortive uprising. The government had granted to Edwards and his colonists, land already occupied by Mexicans.
Instead of seeking to rectify that error, the Edwards group
proceeded to establish themselves on the disputed land. Negotiations proved fruitless, for the Mexican authorities reaffirmed the legitimacy of the original grants made to Mexicans, and annulled Edwards' contract. It must be granted
that the problem originated through a government blunder,
compounded subsequently by Edwards' arrogance. He issued
a series of bombastic, angry pronouncements attacking the
Mexican people and complaining of the wrongdoings of
"this imbecile, this faithless and perfidious government.
Great God! can you any longer hesitate, fellow citizens,
what to do?"

What to do? Edwards proclaimed a new republic, Fredonia, and called upon the United States, other Anglo-Texans, and Indian tribes for aid. Sufficient aid was not forthcoming and the so-called republic of Fredonia did not last
a month. During this crisis the majority of the Anglo-Texans
remained loyal, but the actions of the Edwards' faction
helped to cast further doubts on the practicality of inviting
any more foreigners to Texas.

Nor were matters helped any when it was learned, in
1829, that the United States Government intended to offer

$1,000,000 to purchase Texas and thus to push its national boundary south to the Rio Grande. The Mexican Government was incensed, and while Ambassador Poinsett wisely had not formally presented the offer, the Mexican officials knew about it and the damage was done.

The very next year a new crisis emerged. President Anastasio Bustamante signed an act which aroused the ire of the Anglo-Texans. Reflecting the concern of the Mexican elite over the unhappy developments in Texas, the new legislation was aimed directly at Anglo-Texans and at the United States. The act provided for a cessation of further land grants and for closing the frontier to Anglo-American immigrants. From that moment on it forbade slaves to be brought into Texas. And it provided for customs houses to facilitate the supervision and collection of duties on foreign merchandise coming in through Texas ports. To enforce the act, General Mier y Terán with 1,300 soldiers crossed the Rio Grande and took up posts in a number of locations.

Calling a halt to further land grants was not too disturbing to the Anglo-Texans, who were infuriated, however, by the other provisions of the new law. No more immigrants from the United States! No more slaves to be brought in! Taxes on imports! The last measure was especially aggravating. Under the empresario system, colonists were permitted to import goods from the United States expressly for the purpose of building up the settlements. The newcomers had taken advantage of the laxness of Mexican authorities by importing large quantities of duty-free goods which they used for commercial purposes and not for colony building. The new law placed heavy taxes on all goods coming from the United States; merchandise from other countries was not subject to the tax.

Nor did the Anglo-Texans cherish the presence of Mexican soldiers, for they had enjoyed the privilege of maintaining their own local militia. The soldiers were a miserable bunch of ex-convicts, vagabonds and other miscreants forcibly called to the service of their country. Once in Texas, they committed one outrage after another. In 1832 at Nacogdoches, Velasco, and Anahuac, Texans and Mexicans fought pitched battles.

Then Santa Anna came into the picture. He executed a small-scale "revolution" against President Bustamante, put in his man Gómez Pedraza, came forth as a champion of justice and effected the withdrawal of the Mexican forces from Texas. The Anglo-Texans saw in Santa Anna a great friend to whom they could be loyal.

The clash of the two cultures, the many misunderstandings, the open and secret violations of laws by the Anglo-Texans, the condescending attitude toward Mexicans, the ineptitude of an unstable government, the growing ambitions of frustrated, yet enterprising pioneers, mutual mistrust—all combined to lead to open hostility, open rebellion, and finally, war.

In 1835, Santa Anna, now President of Mexico, abrogated the 1824 constitution. His new constitution provided for a highly centralized government and eliminated all the states' rights so dear to the Anglos. They reacted by setting up a provisional government and driving out the Mexican garrison stationed in San Antonio. The war for secession was on.

The Mexican view is simple enough. The government was faced with the secession of a very large territory. It had to confront fifteen to twenty thousand arrogant Anglo-Americans who, during their fourteen years of colonizing, had given nothing but trouble and now had raised the standard of revolt.

Not long after fighting erupted, Santa Anna personally assumed command of the Mexican forces. The wealthy hacendado had participated in momentous events since the earliest days of the Republic. He was a consummate political actor who, in military matters, provided instances of bravery that alternated with prime examples of cowardice. This scheming, corrupt, wily opportunist, whose mind was filled with dreams of becoming dictator, was the most capable of Mexican officers. His misdeeds remain great blots of shame in the history of Mexico.

The new commander-in-chief headed forces that far outnumbered the Texans. However his army was poorly disciplined with little or no training, and officers were schooled in European methods of fighting ill-suited for the Texas plains. Santa Anna won battles, but lost the war to an ill-equipped, makeshift army of brave, dedicated fighters commanded by brilliant leaders. All the Texans were volunteers, including some Mexicans who also believed in the cause of an independent Texas.

It was in the battles that Santa Anna won that he conducted himself most disgracefully. Near San Antonio stood an old, abandoned Spanish mission, San Antonio de Valero, called the Alamo by the Anglos. Its walls encompassed an area of about fifty by one hundred fifty yards; within them was a half-demolished church, a two-story convent with a large patio, and several thick stone rooms used as a jail. The walls were made of adobe bricks piled eight feet high and three feet thick. The Alamo served as a fortress for 181 Anglo-Texas defenders against an army of four or five thousand infantrymen, horsemen and artillerymen led by His Excellency, Santa Anna.

The siege began on February 23. On March 6 the Mexicans attacked. The fighting was over in one and a half hours.

Two very different portraits of the Mexican
general and dictator, Santa Anna.

Santa Anna admitted that he had lost 600 killed and wounded. His private secretary, Ramón Caro, after he was captured at the battle of San Jacinto, gave the more accurate estimate: "We brought to San Antonio more than 5,000 men and we lost during the siege 1,544 of the best of them. The Texans fought more like devils than like men." Santa Anna's costly victory had to be measured in terms of the very large number of men killed and wounded and also in the loss of morale among the survivors.

The shame lies not only in poor generalship, but also in Santa Anna's disgraceful conduct. Why do Texans, to this day, remember the Alamo? Starting on the very first day of the siege Santa Anna had made it known that no quarter was to be given, no negotiations for an honorable surrender considered. The red flag signalling "No Quarter!" was flown from the tower of a neighboring church. And on the day of the frontal assault, the buglers sounded the *desaguello,* the chilling no quarter call. When the Mexican troops charged into the mission buildings they slaughtered all the survivors, including the wounded, save for a few women and children. The dead were thrown on pyres and burned on Santa Anna's orders. "Remember the Alamo!" became the rallying cry of Texans for the rest of the revolution.

At Goliad, about three hundred Texans surrendered to a superior force commanded by General José Urrea. Urrea was censured by Santa Anna for taking prisoners and ordered that they be summarily executed. The prisoners were marched out into a field, ignorant of their fate, to be butchered by the Mexican soldiers. Wounded were bayoneted; the few who ran away were hunted down and shot. Four doctors and a few others were spared. As at the Alamo, the bodies of the dead were burned.

The two bloody massacres, the merciless killing of prisoners, shocked everyone. Santa Anna's infamous conduct was condemned by Mexican men of good will. However many Mexicans feel that Santa Anna's cruelty has been blown up out of proportion by Texans, for whom "Remember the Alamo!" brings to mind a distorted picture in which all Mexicans are considered a cowardly, untrustworthy, cruel people. Mexicans are quick to acknowledge the crimes of Santa Anna, but quite understandably resent the stereotyping of all Mexicans because of the actions of one contemptible figure.

Santa Anna's army was annihilated and he himself captured at the battle of San Jacinto. The revolution was a success and Texas became an independent republic. His Excellency agreed to treaty terms which set Texas free, but the Mexicans never recognized as legitimate the secession of that vast piece of her land. *No treaty was signed, nor any boundaries fixed.*

For Texans the bitter memories of the slaughter at the Alamo and at Goliad were kept alive by word of mouth, and the stories soon degenerated into myth and falsehood as they were retold from generation to generation. "Texans could not get it out of their heads," wrote historian Erna Fergusson, "that their manifest destiny was to kill Mexicans and take over Mexico."

Texas-Mexicans, on the other hand, who had suffered humiliating treatment at the hands of the Anglo-Americans from the very beginning, now were to suffer new indignities. The sins of Santa Anna were senselessly and brutally visited upon Texas-Mexicans without let-up, and have continued to the present day. There were some exceptions. The *ricos,* considered "good Mexicans," were called *Tejanos* and were permitted, for a while, to play a role in politics and even in the Texas army.

From the time of the establishment of the Republic of Texas until the outbreak of the war between Mexico and the United States ten years later, there were constant border clashes between Mexicans and Texans. Such outrages as raids, arson, murders, rapes, rustling were committed by both forces—uninterrupted guerilla warfare at its worst.

Much of the fighting took place in the disputed area that lies between the Nueces and Rio Grande rivers. For more than a century the Nueces had been the southern boundary of Texas. The Texans ignored this fact and considered the more southern Rio Grande as their southern boundary. In that rather barren region lived Mexicans who were caught between the two fires and were subjected to brutalities by both sides. Raiding parties sometimes became very large-

A Texas caricature of Generalíssimo Santa Anna in 1846. The town is Matamoros.

scale operations, as in the instance when General Vásquez with five hundred men captured San Antonio, Goliad and Refugio in March, 1842; the Mexicans stayed only a few days before withdrawing. In 1841–42, an expedition of 320 Texans, including adventurers from all over the United States, and a few from other countries, invaded New Mexico. Part of the force was killed by Kiowa Indians; the remainder was captured by General Manuel Armijo, then Governor of New Mexico. Those captured were marched to Mexico City and imprisoned there.

In September, 1842, General Adrian Woll and one thousand Mexican soldiers again occupied San Antonio, and after being defeated by a hastily gathered Texan force, withdrew to the other side of the Rio Grande. The Texans retaliated in November when General Alexander Somervell and 750 adventurous rabble captured Laredo. The men plundered the town but Somervell compelled them to return the loot. Two hundred chagrined malcontents then quit. Not long after, Somervell and 250 more returned to Texas while the remaining 300, commanded by Colonel William Fisher, went on to attack the small town of Mier, just south of the Rio Grande. They were defeated in a battle with 1,700 Mexicans to whom they surrendered. About 100 of the prisoners were executed or died, 25 escaped and the balance of 121 were released.

All these incidents and more were but the prelude to the war between Mexico and the United States, precipitated when Texas was annexed in March, 1845. Disagreement persists among historians about whether the United States was engaged in a just war. At the time, many North Americans as well as Texans were enthusiastic over the opportunity to "have a crack" at the Mexicans, whom they had come to despise. A few lone voices were raised in protest.

A section of the Alamo ruins depicting the
walls that served for defense.

Among them were Abraham Lincoln, Congressman from
Illinois; Thomas Corwin, Senator from Ohio; and Henry
David Thoreau, writer. On the floor of the Senate, Corwin
speaking against the appropriations bill, denounced the war
as one that President Polk had forced upon Mexico, and
ridiculed those expansionists who cried for more room, saying: "If I were a Mexican I would tell you: Have you not
room in your own country to bury your dead men? If you
come into Mexico we will greet you with bloody hands and

welcome you to hospitable graves." Thoreau refused to pay taxes for the prosecution of an unjust war and for this act of civil disobedience * was jailed. During his short stay in prison he was visited by his friend, Ralph Waldo Emerson, who exclaimed, "Henry, what are you doing in there?" To which Thoreau replied, "Ralph, what are you doing out there?"

For three decades there had been conflict in Texas, major responsibility for which is placed upon the Anglo-Texans. These newcomers had flaunted the law, derided Mexicans, and conducted themselves as conquerors in a land to which they had been invited. They had rebelled and established a republic never recognized by Mexico. They had flirted constantly with the expansionism of their original homeland, the United States. The United States, through a number of declarations by officials and through unfriendly actions, had made it abundantly clear that it aimed at conquering part, if not all, of Mexico. Following the annexation of Texas, the United States was looking for any pretext to commence war against Mexico.

The opportunity came when United States troops crossed the Nueces river. Texas had considered its border rightfully to be the Rio Grande. Mexico considered the Nueces to be the border and therefore viewed its crossing as an invasion. The first shots were fired by Mexican troops led by General Mariano Arista, who had crossed the Rio Grande in an effort to drive the Americans back to the Nueces. President Polk declared that Mexicans had invaded the territory of the United States and that therefore war had broken out.

The disgraced Santa Anna returned from exile in 1846 to become President and Generalissimo and went on to lead his country to an ignominious defeat.

---

* Thoreau's civil disobedience inspired Gandhi in India and subsequently Martin Luther King and César Chávez in the United States.

Authentic accounts describe the conduct of the American troops, most of whom were volunteers. According to General Winfield Scott they "had committed atrocities to make Heaven weep and every American of Christian morals blush for his country. Murder, robbery and rape of mothers and daughters in the presence of tied-up males of the families have been common all along the Rio Grande." What a way to remember the Alamo! Another officer, then Lieutenant George G. Meade, later to be a famous Civil War general, charged that the volunteers were "driving husbands out of houses and raping their wives . . . they are a set of Goths and Vandals without discipline, making us a terror to innocent people." They were charged with outrageous anti-Catholic actions, such as drinking out of holy vessels and desecrating churches. The hatred thus engendered remains part of a bitter heritage for Mexicans and Mexican-Americans.

The bitterness was enhanced when the terms of the peace Treaty of Guadalupe Hidalgo, signed February, 1848, became known. Mexico had to give up its claims to Texas and was given an indemnity of $15,000,000 for all the rest of its territory west to the Pacific. The acquisition of New Mexico, Arizona, California, Utah, Nevada and the southern part of Colorado made quite clear the imperialist drive of the United States. There was abundant evidence that the larger aims were premeditated; the victory in the war over Texas provided the excuse for the giant of the north to extend its southern holdings at the expense of Mexico. The conquest of the Indians and of their land by the Spaniards and Mexicans was followed by the conquest of the Mexicans by the Anglo-Americans.

> History is not woven with inno-
> cent hands. Among all the causes
> which degrade and demoralize
> men, power is the most constant
> and active.
>
> Lord Acton

## CHAPTER VI

# Strangers in Their Own Land

FOR THE FIRST TIME IN ITS HISTORY THE UNITED STATES acquired by conquest land inhabited by an ethnic minority other than Indians. The thorny question of the status of the Mexican population was given careful consideration by the treaty makers. Despite their humble position at the treaty table, the Mexican representatives were successful in obtaining provisions in the treaty to protect their former citizens. Since those provisions are both historically important and also have considerable relevance for the contemporary scene, the two pertinent articles are given in full:

### ARTICLE VIII

Mexicans now established in territories previously belonging to Mexico, and which remain for the future within the limits of the United States, as defined by the present treaty, shall be free to continue where they now reside, or to remove at any time to the Mexican Republic, retaining the property which they possess in the said territories, or disposing thereof, and removing the proceeds wher-

106

ever they please; without their being subjected, on this account, to any contribution, tax or charge whatever. Those who shall prefer to remain in the said territories, may either retain the title and rights of Mexican citizens, or acquire those of citizens of the United States. But they shall be under the obligation to make their election within one year from the date of the exchange of ratifications of this treaty: and those who shall remain in the said territories, after the expiration of that year, without having declared their intention to retain the character of Mexicans, shall be considered to become citizens of the United States.

In the said territories, property of every kind, now belonging to Mexicans, not established there, shall be inviolably respected. The present owners, the heirs of these, and all Mexicans who may hereafter acquire said property by contract, shall enjoy with respect to it, guaranties equally ample as if the same belonged to citizens of the United States.

ARTICLE IX

The Mexicans who, in the territories aforesaid, shall not preserve the character of citizens of the Mexican Republic, conformably with what is stipulated in the preceding article, shall be incorporated into the Union of the United States and be admitted, at the proper time (to be judged by the Congress of the United States) to the enjoyment of all the rights of citizens of the United States according to the principles of the Constitution; and in the meantime shall be maintained and protected in the free enjoyment of their liberty and property, and secured in the free exercise of their religion without restriction.

A treaty is a piece of paper. Whether it is translated into action depends upon the good will of the parties concerned.

It was incumbent upon the United States to enforce the provisions that guaranteed the personal and property rights of Mexicans, now Mexican-Americans. Reies López Tijerina, the militant Chicano leader in New Mexico, has committed the two articles to memory, and is quick to point out that the government of the United States has not been conducting itself honorably in this regard. The evidence supports Tijerina. Articles VIII and IX are not more than words on a piece of paper.

California    Before the war with Mexico, it was becoming obvious that the United States had designs on acquiring California. President Jackson, as early as 1835, had indicated his desire to purchase California and more. After Texas seceded from Mexico, Jackson urged the new Republic of Texas to extend its boundaries westward to the Pacific. In 1841 President Tyler authorized several exploratory expeditions, one of which visited the port of San Francisco. The next year Commodore Thomas Ap Catesby Jones, commanding the Pacific squadron, either was falsely informed, or believed a rumor that the United States was at war with Mexico. From Callao, Peru, Jones brought his fleet to Monterey, demanded the city's surrender, and raised the American flag. His apologies two days later did little to mollify the ruffled tempers of the authorities in Mexico City, no less the inhabitants of Monterey.

When Polk became President in 1845, the expansionism implicit in the doctrine of *Manifest Destiny* was made explicit. He encouraged a separatist movement in California which was almost on the verge of success in 1846 when an unexpected event interfered with the carefully laid plans of Polk's agents in California. The war with Mexico put an end to such subterfuges or the need for them.

Nine days before the Treaty of Guadalupe Hidalgo was signed, gold was discovered in California. Gold! The centuries-old dream of the Spaniards was realized. When the Mexicans signed the treaty giving away California, they had not yet learned of the momentous discovery. Neither Spaniards nor Mexicans were to benefit from the belated gold find.

The discovery of gold gave rise to a gold rush in 1848, followed by a stampede in 1849. During the first months, the rush emptied towns and cities in northern California. Among the first to reach the gold fields were Mexican-Americans.

During that first year there were few serious incidents among the 1,300 Californios and the 4,000 Yankees. Some Californios, like Antonio Coronel, a Mexican school teacher, struck it rich, but when he returned on a second trip in 1849 he struck trouble.

In 1849, a gold-crazed horde of people of every calling— adventurers, prospectors, merchants, vagabonds, pickpockets, assassins, ex-farmers, ex-clerks, journalists, prostitutes, dance-hall girls, saloon keepers, rich and poor, innocents and villains—poured into California from the United States, from Europe, from Latin America and even from China.

It is doubtful that the Yankees had heard about Articles VIII and IX of the Treaty of Guadalupe Hidalgo. It is also doubtful that they knew that California had been part of Mexico, and that there were native Californians whose roots in the state went back two hundred years and more. What they did know was that California was part of the United States, and "greasers" had no place there. The forty-niners made no distinctions between Californios and Mexicans, Peruvians and Chileans. They were all foreigners, all "greasers" or "dirty Mex." The few Californios plus the 8,000 Mexicans were in no position to discuss matters calmly with the 80,000 Yankee newcomers, so many of whom were ugly racists.

Californios were amazed to see posters announcing that foreigners had no right to be in or near the mines and that they had to leave at once. Nor did it matter that the Californios were not foreigners. Incident piled upon ugly incident. Coronel gave five pounds of gold to ransom a colleague accused by Yankees of stealing that amount. The money was accepted. Then the mob of hundreds pronounced five prisoners guilty and witnessed their flogging. Two men, a Chilean and a Frenchman, neither of whom had understood the bizarre proceedings conducted in English, were

Sutter's Fort, near Sacramento City, at the time of the gold rush.

first whipped and then lynched. That was the first lynching in California, U.S.A., and the site where it took place was appropriately named Hangtown.

Vigilantes at famous Sutter's mill, convinced that their preposterous statement of "no trespass" was legal, forced hundreds of Spanish-speaking folk to leave the area. Coronel and most other Californios decided that discretion was superior to a quixotic valor and returned to their homes.

Other Latin Americans persisted in staying despite the ugly climate. Most of them were from Mexico; some from Chile and Peru. Many of the Mexicans were not miners. From Sonora came many traders offering for sale pack mules, mining supplies, and vegetables. At first, for almost three years, these immigrants were welcome, their offerings eagerly awaited. But opposition by Yankee traders called a halt to such enterprise; Yankees could be enterprising, not "greasers." The miners among the group, after continually being insulted and subjected to repeated acts of violence, finally gave up. That included many Mexicans who had been working as common laborers in the mines and in the mining towns. While some were making the long trek back to Sonora, they were robbed of their few belongings, including their horses and mules, so that they had to continue the journey, even across the desert, on foot. The Chileans and Peruvians fled to the ports to embark on ships that would return them to their native lands where they discouraged their countrymen from going to California, land of the gold-crazed "gringos."

The California legislature passed a miners' license tax directed at the foreign miner in general and the Mexican in particular. In the course of collecting the tax, "volunteer" tax collectors vandalized and burned property, and physically attacked Mexicans. At Sonora an inflamed mob of two thousand American miners attacked a camp of Mexicans. They killed many, burned the camp to the ground and rounded up hundreds of men, women and children to be driven like so many animals into a stockade.

One of the ironies giving added emphasis to the tragedy is that the very method of creek-bed or placer mining first used in California was Mexican. For centuries the Sonorans had been using the *batea,* a shallow bowl or pan into which water, and dirt or gravel, possibly containing grains of gold, were placed. Carefully swishing the contents in a sort of circular motion, the prospector would sift out the dirt, pebbles and other worthless matter, leaving a few grains of the heavier gold on the bottom. This was the method universally used in California during the gold rush.

In the areas of southern California where there was little or no water in the gold fields, the Mexicans perfected the "dry-wash" technique, a method that was also widely used by the Anglo-Americans who drove off their teachers and monopolized the diggings.

Experienced gold prospectors soon learned that the gold they panned in creek beds was just a minor amount, and had usually washed out from a larger ledge or deposit near the head of the stream. Gold ore was found in quartz. Quartz mining technique had been perfected by Mexicans long familiar with quartz ores in their own country. That technique too was borrowed by the Yankee who had had no experience in such mining procedure.

One other mining technique of great importance was borrowed from the Mexicans. Silver, as well as gold, was located in California and elsewhere in the Southwest. The process involved in extracting silver from its ore was invented by a Mexican, Bartolomé de Medina, in 1557. Called the *patio* process (See p. 25) it required the use of quicksilver, or mercury. In 1845, Captain Andrés Castillero accidentally discovered a mercury mine in the mountains twelve miles from San José, California. The use of mercury coming from this mine, called New Almadén after the famous Almadén mine in Spain, made possible the more efficient and more economical exploitation of the silver mines in the Southwest. Castillero sold his rights at the outbreak of the Mexican war to some Britons and Americans. They sent their engineers to Spain to study the process of mining mercury, and they employed mostly Mexican laborers who had the requisite skills.

The technical terms used in mining were Spanish, and since there were no English equivalents for many of them, the anti-Spanish Yankees had to use the Spanish language.

How did the big rancheros fare? For the first three years, while the gold rush was at its height, the cattle and sheep ranches were not disturbed. On the contrary, the wave of migration into California proved an economic boom for the stockmen. But with the passage of the Federal Land Law of 1851, they too were victimized.

The holders of the land grants made during Mexican and even during Spanish days were suddenly confronted with unforeseen problems. Boundaries had not been too carefully established; in point of fact they were quite vague. Deeds had been lost, some transferred. Some owners had only their residence of many decades as proof. Ostensibly the new land law of 1851 had as its chief purpose to sort out the valid from the worthless claims.

What were the consequences? By the 1880's the Californios held but one-quarter of the land they had possessed before the Treaty of Guadalupe Hidalgo. In *Progress and Poverty,* Henry George tersely described what happened as a "history of greed, of perjury, of corruption, of spoliation and high-handed robbery." The thirty years between the passage of the law in 1851 and the 1880's were filled with costly litigation, swindling, cheating, financial manipulations, and armed struggles which resulted in the transfer of the bulk of the land to Anglo-Americans.

In the political arena, Californios, for a while, held offices at the town, city, county and state levels. In some instances they held the majority of positions in towns and counties. But as the influx of Anglo-Americans grew, the political power of the native Californians declined. By the 1880's it was a rarity for a Californio to hold any important political offices, whether by election or by appointment. The Anglo-Americans comprised an overwhelming majority of the population and therefore they dominated the political scene to the point where ethnic minorities were eased out.

While frontier life still existed in California, frontier lawlessness flourished. An era of banditry, highly romanticized in Hollywood films, accompanied frontier conditions. Bandits came in all shapes and sizes, but the supremacist Americans took for granted that all bandits were Mexican. Of the many, one stands out in history and is a hero to Mexican-Americans today. Novels, films, short stories, poetry and many songs and ballads have been written about Joaquín. Oddly enough, there is dispute whether there in fact was a Joaquín. A number of surnames have been attributed to this folk hero; the most popular is Murieta.

So many tales have been spun about this Robin Hood that there must have been more than one; the composite is clearly a work of fiction. Putting all the stories together one learns that Joaquín was in several different places at precisely the same time. As fiction has it, he killed evildoers and robbed the rich to give to the poor.

Many of those robbed and murdered were Chinese, large numbers of whom had been brought in to replace the despised Mexicans as laborers. The spate of crimes reached such a pitch, and so many robbery-murders were pinned on Joaquín that a substantial reward was set and several vigilante and other volunteer groups attempted to hunt him down. In the course of these manhunts, many an innocent Mexican along with guilty bandits were summarily punished with the "justice" of the gun and the rope.

One group of ranger-like men commanded by a former army officer, Captain Harry S. Love, garnered the reward of $5,000 provided by the state legislature. Love's group had a gun fight with some Mexican horsemen they encountered on the trail. Two Mexicans were killed; Love identified one as Joaquín and the other as his chief aide, three-fingered Jack García. How Captain Love was able to make a positive identification on the basis of the very vague descriptions current is subject to considerable doubt. Love brought in, as proof, the three-fingered hand of García and the head he had hacked off the other Mexican. The head was pickled, and put on display in a saloon in San Francisco (one story locates the head in a museum in that city) only to disappear during the great earthquake of 1906.

Killing the real—or imaginary Joaquín—in 1853 did not end banditry in California. Nor did it end the hunting down of Mexicans, bandits or otherwise, for another twenty years. However by the 1870's, highway robberies, and other such exploits of banditry, had become pretty much a thing of the past.

The legendary exploits of Joaquín find a responsive chord in the hearts of some Mexican-Americans today. For them he exemplifies the free, bold, brave Robin Hood who had *machismo,* that hard-to-define special quality of virility and dignity that distinguish the independent free-spirited man from the humble and subservient one.

**New Mexico**   Like California, New Mexico was easily conquered by the United States. Colonel Stephen Watts Kearney was able to take the territory without firing a shot. The Anglo-Americans who had already settled in the area had paved the way, so to speak, for the bloodless surrender. Furthermore, the rich families of New Mexico were divided over the question of resistance. They lacked adequate arms, and the Governor, General Manuel Armijo, was more interested in preserving his interest in the ongoing Santa Fe trade. With Mexico far away, physically and politically, it seemed wise to accept the military occupation.

The occupying forces were made up of volunteers who proceeded to conduct themselves as arrogant conquerors. Santa Fe was filled with drunken, boisterous brawlers who would not withhold their contempt and blind hatred of Mexicans. That source of discontent was increased when rumors circulated that Americans were going to confiscate land, and that all land would be taxed. Opposition to American rule grew and a plot was hatched among the *ricos* and the clergy of Santa Fe and Taos. The clergy believed, with justification, that they would be deprived of their special privileges and power. The conspirators planned their uprising for Christmas Eve of 1846 and intended to assassinate Governor Charles Bent and other prominent Americans. The plot was uncovered in time and the ringleaders arrested.

However, on January 17, 1847 a revolt did materialize. Taos Indians and Mexicans still loyal to Mexico revolted in Taos and in Mora. Bent was assassinated and several other Americans were killed before the insurgents were defeated by American troops. An interesting sidelight of the revolt is the speculation that it had been masterminded by a priest, José Antonio Martínez. Father Martínez had been the priest at Taos since 1822 and had gained a reputation of being honest—a sage, free-wheeling independent, a liberal, and a reformer. He introduced a school for girls as well as for boys. He trained the sons of the rich, many of whom subsequently became important political figures in New Mexico. He published and edited the first newspaper in the territory, *El Crépusculo de la Libertad (The Dawn of Liberty)*. The Taos Indians adored him and had followed his leadership in a revolt in 1837 when the Santa Fe government was overthrown. This later revolt of the Taos Indians, January, 1847, seemed to have the earmarks of the leadership of Padre Martínez. But because nothing could be proved, or perhaps because he was too important a figure and a member of one of the richest landowning families, he was not accused openly nor arrested. However Bishop Lamy suspended Father Martínez, who ignored the suspension, functioning as priest in Taos until his death in 1867. The church hierarchy did not tolerate dissenters, especially if they were close to the people. The Bishop excommunicated, a few years later, another religious leader of the people, Father Gallegos. Lacking faith in Mexican priests, the Church for some time sent French, German and Belgian priests to serve in New Mexico.

Because there was little migration of Americans into New Mexico, the Spanish-speaking contingent remained a majority for many decades. Therefore the Americans preferred to rule New Mexico as a territory, employing a variety of political strategems to delay the achievement of statehood until 1912. The American minority obtained the key appointive posts in the territory, while the Mexican-American majority had to settle for relatively minor, elective positions.

A powerful friend of the Americans in Congress was the famous Thaddeus Stevens. Stevens had fought the good fight during post-Civil War days on behalf of the newly freed Negroes of the South. However, like so many heroes, Stevens had his quota of virulent prejudice. The Congressman informed his colleagues that in New Mexico, "The mass of the people are Mexicans, a hybrid race of Spanish and Indian origin, ignorant, degraded, demoralized and priest-ridden." Such violent anti-Mexican bias brings into question his vaunted support of the freedmen, a support which was inspired, most probably, solely for political and not humanitarian reasons. His motives for supporting the Anglo-American clique in New Mexico were certainly not humanitarian.

Inasmuch as the majority of the members of the territorial legislature were wealthy Mexican-Americans, the Americans conveniently forged a loose alliance with them. Actually it was an alliance of the rich. The *ricos,* intent on preserving their land grants and the system of peonage, combined with the Anglo-American bankers, merchants, lawyers and politicians to exercise effective control over economic and political affairs.

The Anglo-American portion of the cabal became known as "the Santa Fe Ring" which, along with *ricos,* "manipulated the Indian Bureau; controlled the allocation of contracts to supply the army posts; dictated territorial appointments; and exercised a great influence over the courts," writes Carey McWilliams in his path-breaking book, *North From Mexico.* The Ring became more than one, for in time there was a Cattle Ring, a Mining Ring, a Public Land Stealing Ring and others designed to benefit a few clever, greedy Anglo-Americans.

This peculiar alliance, which also benefitted some rich Mexican-Americans, had results which differentiate the ethnic history of New Mexico sharply from what happened in California and in Texas. The hatred between the Spanish-speaking majority and the Anglo-American minority was minimized. In the political area, Mexican-Americans shared with Anglos, almost on a fifty-fifty basis, offices at the city, county, state and even federal level. The latent antagonism manifested itself sharply only in recent years, but it has never reached the degree of virulence that prevails in Texas and in California.

As in California, the *ricos* were unable to keep all of the huge Spanish and Mexican land grants. By 1900 about eighty percent had found its way into the hands of lawyers, American settlers and some English land-speculating companies. Some acquired tremendous holdings. For example, Thomas B. Catron, one of the top leaders of the Santa Fe Ring, *admitted* to an estate consisting of more than 250,000 acres. An unofficial estimate at the time put Catron's holdings to be 2,000,000 acres and stated that he was part owner or attorney for 4,000,000 more.

The stakes being so high, corruption and even murder accompanied the disposal of the land grants and of the public land. What the kings of Spain had acquired by force and had distributed with such largesse, now was transferred to private owners through the more subtle and sophisticated methods of the nineteenth century. The record of Spain's conquests is open. The transfer of land titles in the nineteenth century is semi-hidden in legal, court, and governmental archives; and much of the history of the land steals will never be known for it never reached any printed pages.

Texas cattlemen had long eyed the open expanses of New Mexican land. As large as Texas itself is, with more grazing land than that of all France, there was no limit to the greed of the Texas stockmen. After the Civil War the expansion into New Mexico developed rapidly and with it came the range wars between cattlemen and sheepmen, between Anglos and Hispanos. The Mexican sheepmen grazed their flocks in open, unfenced pastures. There was never any serious conflict over grazing rights and any mixups of sheep were easily and efficiently straightened out. The Texas cattlemen, starting in 1875, brought in barbed wire fencing, an action which touched off endless guerrilla war between the two rival interests. The cowboys and the gunmen hired by the cattle ranchers shot up towns, burned scores of farm buildings, and hanged and shot dozens of Spanish-speaking people while suffering not a few casualties themselves.

The sheepmen sent out masked, white-hooded riders (the *Gorras Blancas*) who cut barbed wire and burned corrals and barns. But they were outnumbered and eventually many lost their pastures to the Texans working with the Santa Fe Ring. Still, some *ricos* held on to large tracts of land and remained owners of great flocks of sheep. There were no longer such fabulous holdings like that of Bartolomé Baca, a Spanish governor whose flocks totalled two million, or even like that of "El Guero" Chávez, the first governor after Mexico became a republic, who owned one million sheep. However some private holdings were as large as 250,000 acres and with tens of thousands, perhaps hundreds of thousands, of sheep.

**Arizona** What is now called Arizona was part of the New Mexican territory. This western portion, which became known by its present name in 1856, had remained rough frontier land for a longer time than any other region of the far Southwest. It was the principal stronghold of the Apaches, who had never ceased fighting against all comers. The incessant raids of the Apaches created a bond of mutual defense between the Mexican-Americans and the few Anglos. For the first few decades after the war with Mexico, relations between these two peoples were friendly.

These amicable relations came to an end in the 1880's. Silver, gold and copper had been discovered as early as the 1850's in the southern area—part of the Gadsden Purchase.* Fantastically rich lodes were discovered in 1877. By 1889, two transcontinental railroads crossed the Arizona territory. To meet the rising needs for beef and leather, the cattle industry grew spectacularly.

Mines, railroads, and cattle meant an influx of migrants —ranchers, cowboys, merchants, roughnecks, conspirators, murderers, racists, counsellors. Most of the stock in Arizona had been sheep. Now the incoming cattlemen, mainly from Texas, competed with the sheep men for land and that kind of competition meant range wars, rustling, arson, murders, and lynchings. The Texas cowboys brought to Arizona their hatred of "greasers," a hatred which exploded into violence without the slightest provocation.

During the building of the Southern Pacific Railway, several thousand Mexican laborers were employed. When the railroad no longer needed them, they were discharged and about 1500 of them elected to stay on in Phoenix. Their presence was resented by the Anglos who found ways to make life miserable for them.

Texas    Unlike the situation in California or in New Mexico, in Texas the Anglo-Americans outnumbered the Mexicans from the beginning; by 1847 there were about 100,000

---

* Gadsden Purchase: In 1853, the U.S.A. purchased for $10,000,000 the area bounded on the north by the Gila River, extending from the Colorado in the west to the Rio Grande in the east, and the present southern boundary with Mexico. This region was purchased for its suitability for a projected transcontinental railroad.

of the former compared to only 4,000 of the latter, most of whom were concentrated in the south near the border. Most of the anti-Mexican "incidents" took place in the narrow strip south of the Nueces river.

When the Treaty of Guadalupe Hidalgo was being negotiated, the Mexicans sought to have inserted a provision barring slavery in the territory ceded to the United States. Their attempt was unsuccessful, however, for the slave-holding states were too powerful to permit such a blow to their way of life.

Negro slaves in Texas made use of the opportunity afforded by the proximity of the Mexican border and profited from aid given by the anti-slave Mexicans. As early as 1839, Texas slave owners were complaining that large numbers of fugitives were crossing the Rio Grande. A large colony of ex-slaves developed in Matamoros. In 1856 two insurrectionary schemes were thwarted. In Colorado County, it was alleged that two hundred slaves, aided by one white American and a number of Mexicans, were conspiring to rebel and to escape. The Mexicans and the one American were ordered to leave the country. The Blacks were severely whipped; two of them died and three were hanged. In November a slave revolt in Lavaca, DeWitt and Victoria counties was betrayed and again Mexicans were implicated. Indignant Texans complained that the very presence of Mexican peóns "is an intolerable nuisance" and that they were a permanent threat to the institution of slavery.

The next year federal troops had to be called in to protect Mexicans engaged in hauling freight on ox-carts from the coast and from Chihuahua to San Antonio. Envious Texans were raiding the cart trains, stealing the cargo and killing the drivers. Following several protests by the Mexican ambassador, Washington sent in troops to protect the Mexican carters.

Blood flowed along the Rio Grande again when a Brownsville-born, wealthy Mexican started a sort of private war against "gringos." Juan Nepomuceno Cortina, popularly known as Ceno and called "the red robber of the Rio Grande" (the "red" in the title derived from his red beard) for fifteen years led his band in a war against the Anglos to defend his countrymen against the injustices committed against them.

This Robin Hood was not merely a cattle thief and bandit, but conducted guerrilla warfare throughout the length and breadth of the valley of the lower Rio Grande. In 1859 he led his private army in an invasion of Brownsville where five Americans were killed, Mexican prisoners were released from jail, and shops were looted. Texas Rangers illegally pursued Cortina and his band across the Rio Grande and the two groups clashed in an indecisive battle at Las Cuevas.

Cortina issued manifestoes in which he exposed the machinations of Anglo lawyers who, he alleged, were participating in robbing Mexicans of their lands. In one such proclamation he wrote:

> Mexicans! Is there no remedy for you? Inviolable laws, yet useless, serve, it is true, certain judges and hypocritical authorities, cemented in evil and injustice, to do whatever suits them, and to satisfy their vile avarice at the cost of your patience and suffering; rising in their frenzy, even to the taking of life, through the treacherous hands of their bailiffs . . . .

His flamboyant career came to an end when dictator Porfirio Díaz arrested him in 1873.

"Robin Hoods" may do much to keep hope alive, but such individualistic actions, no matter how heroic and self-sacrificing, do little in the way of resolving basic problems.

For several decades after the Treaty of Guadalupe Hidalgo, Mexicans could not conceive of Texas being foreign territory; it had been Mexican for three hundred years. The border was an artificial boundary which Mexicans and Americans crossed in the most routine way. So did cattle, which knew nothing about international borders. The possibilities for "incidents" were made to order for whomever wished to capitalize on real or alleged violations. In the years after the American Civil War, rustling on both sides of the Rio Grande was commonplace. So was banditry. Raiding parties were alternately Mexican and American. Neither government had respect for the other so that it was often the case that federal troops of both nations crossed the border in violation of international law.

Every Mexican in Texas became suspect. Innocent farmers and stockmen were murdered, buildings were burned, cattle stampeded—one could compile a catalogue of every conceivable crime. Texans hated Mexicans and the feeling was hotly reciprocated.

There is no record of any Texan being tried and convicted for murdering a Mexican. No records were kept of the number of Mexicans who were killed.

In the national periodical, *World's Work,* a reporter stated that "Some of the Rangers have degenerated into man killers. There is no penalty for killing [Mexicans], for no jury along the border would ever convict a white man for shooting a Mexican." There were so many killings of Mexican-Americans by Rangers, and by other Texans, during the early 1920's that *The New York Times* exclaimed in an editorial that "the killing of Mexicans without provocation is so common as to pass unnoticed."

Land titles were challenged, and many an old land title became invalid after court cases decided in favor of American claimants time and time again. When Mexican landowners did win, much of their land was lost anyhow in payment of fees to American lawyers.

From 1848, that is from the time of the secession of the Southwest to the United States, the history of Mexican-Americans was filled with anguish and travail. Articles VIII and IX of the Treaty which promised so much, were never realized. Their land was taken—by force, by chicanery, and by law. Except in New Mexico, Mexican Americans had become political nonentities. Their economic role was minimized, and they were relegated to being servants, common laborers, peóns. Social outcasts, they were denied the right to participate in the cultural and social life of the nation which had forcibly adopted them. They were strangers in what had been their own land for almost three centuries.

Among individuals, as among
nations, respect for the rights
of others is peace.
Benito Juárez

## CHAPTER VII

# Juárez, Zapata and Villa

FOR MANY DECADES AFTER THE ACQUISITION OF THE SOUTH-
west by the United States, events in Mexico were of vital
concern to Mexican-Americans. The umbilical cord which
tied Mexican-Americans to their original homeland was not
to be severed merely by the formal change of national status.

The struggle for reform in Mexico in the 1850's, the
French intervention of the 1860's, the long era of the dictatorship of Porfirio Díaz, the Mexican Revolution that began in 1910 and which in some ways continues to this day,
made profound impressions upon Mexicans living in the
United States.

For many people the memory of a significant historical
occurrence is intimately connected with the life and activities of some outstanding individual. The deeds of some great
man loom far more importantly than all the intricate political, economic and social phenomena with which he is inextricably bound. Prominent in the galaxy of heroes for present day Mexican-Americans are three Mexicans of the past:
Juárez, Zapata and Villa. The actions of the latter two are

connected with the Mexican Revolution of 1910. The life of Juárez is intertwined with the War of Reform and with the French intervention. The achievements and the aspirations of these three Mexicans provide inspiration for many Chicanos today. Of the three, Juárez stands out as one of the most illustrious men of modern times in all the Americas.

Juárez   Benito Juárez was a full-blooded Zapotec Indian born March 21, 1806 in the tiny village of San Pablo Gualatao, not far from the city of Oaxaca, capital of the state of the same name. Orphaned at age three, he was brought up by his uncle, a very poor, hard-working bachelor barely scrounging out a living. Benito helped out by herding sheep and performing other farm chores in the village of no more than one hundred Indian inhabitants. The village nestles on the side of a mountain and encircles a clear, blue, little lake surrounded by trees. The idyllic beauty of the landscape, upon which he could feast his eyes every day, haunted Benito's memories. It was his fondest, but unrealized, hope that he would be able to live out his life amidst the natural splendors of his birthplace.

Two hungers drove him from his lovely sylvan surroundings—the ordinary, physical variety and a hunger for learning. His uncle had taught him to read and to speak some Spanish—enough for the youngster to realize that there was much to learn. There was no school or library in his isolated village. At age twelve he ran away from his home, such as it was.

Although he had started out on foot early in the morning, it was night before he reached Oaxaca, forty miles on the other side of the mountain. After staying a few days with his sister María, a domestic servant, he was fortunate in being befriended by a bookbinder, Antonio Salanueva. Benito served his benefactor as a houseboy but had time to attend a primary school where he improved his reading and learned to write.

After two years, he went to the seminary college to study Latin and Spanish grammar for two more years, followed

Benito Juárez, the Mexican "Abraham Lincoln," as portrayed by the internationally famous muralist, Diego Rivera.

by four years of courses in the arts, passing the required examinations with grades of excellent. Usually any Indian lucky enough to get this much education would have to settle for the priesthood, a goal urged upon him by his uncle. But Juárez, although a devout Catholic, had come to despise the clergy; most were poorly educated, often smug, and he had ample opportunity to observe at firsthand frequent examples of their hypocrisy. Benito's talents impelled him in a different direction.

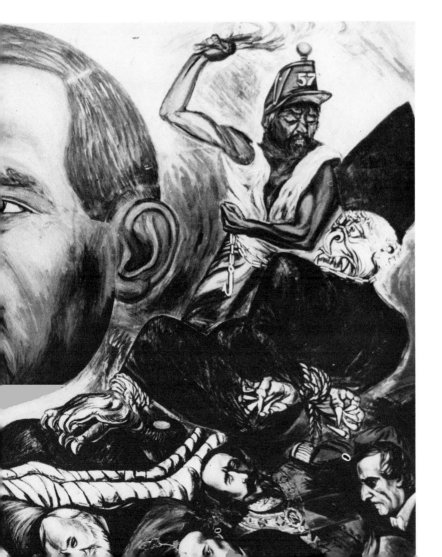

He attended the Institute of Sciences and Arts where he came under the influence of liberal priests and professors. The Institute was a secular school, one of very few at the time, and its liberal philosophy came under constant attack by the church hierarchy and by other conservatives. They called the Institute "a house of prostitution, and the professors and students heretics and libertines."

When he was twenty-five years old, Juárez completed his studies in law, graduating with honors. He began to practice and at the same time he was elected an alderman in Oaxaca.

In 1834 he passed the examination of the State Court of Justice and was entitled "advocate." That same year, the ever courteous and modest Juárez was falsely accused of inciting to riot and was jailed for nine days before being freed on bail. Writing about this experience, many years later, he took the opportunity to expound some fundamentals of his political philosophy:

> These blows that I suffered, and that almost daily I saw suffered by the unprotected who complained of the arbitrary acts of the privileged classes in close association with the civil authority, showed me most clearly that society would never be happy while those classes existed in alliance with the public powers, and confirmed me in my resolution to work unceasingly to destroy the evil power of the privileged classes. This I did as well as I could, and this the liberal party would do; but unluckily for humanity, the remedy that was then being used did not go to the root of the evil, for although many times a reactionary administration was overthrown and replaced by a liberal one, the change was only one of persons, and there remained active in the laws and constitutions the ecclesiastic and military exemptions, religious intolerance, the state religion, and the continued possession by the clergy of numerous properties that they used wrongly to establish firmly their destructive power. Thus it

was that when a liberal administration was established, only a few months later it was overthrown, and its adherents were persecuted.

The key to solving the fundamental problems of the nation, then, was constitutional change. What Juárez was to learn was that to effect such a change in his country, to bring to light a liberal, democratic constitution would require a revolution.

Reference has been made to the chaotic state of affairs that followed the establishment of Mexico as an independent nation. Juárez noted the rapid succession of leaders; a caudillo would pronounce, a Plan would be presented, and a new national government, pledged to law and order, would emerge only to succumb to another caudillo, a pronouncement and a Plan. It was during this time that Juárez was throwing unbounded energy into defending the rights of the oppressed both in his capacity as advocate and as a politician. He held a number of appointive and elected posts at the city and state level for thirteen years, gaining political experience which led to his election in 1847 to the governorship of the state of Oaxaca.

To be a politician, one must make promises. The politician who fulfills his promises is a rarity. The Indian from Oaxaca was just that. Two successive, honest and efficient reform administrations won Juárez the gratitude of the Indians and other poor folk, and the respect of other liberals. At the same time he won the hatred of the conservatives like Santa Anna. When that ubiquitous caudillo returned to power in 1853, it meant the end of liberal administrations in Oaxaca or anywhere else, and for honest Juárez it meant involuntary exile.

After his governorship terminated in August, 1852, he was harassed and persecuted by the reactionaries who had come into national power. Once again he was arrested on the false charge of inciting the townspeople of Etla to riot, held incommunicado for several days, given a passport and ordered into exile to Europe. He was given no opportunity to see his beloved wife and children, who themselves were being hounded by the agents of Santa Anna.

Juárez and several fellow exiles went to Havana but instead of going on to Europe, they sailed to New Orleans where many other exiled Mexicans were living—and plotting. The future president shared a garret with a friend, José María Maza, in a boardinghouse where another close friend, the brilliant intellectual, Melchor Ocampo, also lived. They earned a living by making and selling cigarettes and cigars. From the proceeds they bought milk and black bread, a meagre diet occasionally supplemented by fish caught in the Mississippi. The daily sight of black slaves affected Juárez emotionally and politically. He mentally reaffirmed his vow to seek the abolition of all forms of servitude in Mexico.

The physical misery was augmented by the mental torment of Juárez the family man anxious about his wife and children, and the torment of Juárez the citizen concerned about the fate of his country. Santa Anna's rule daily became more tyrannical, producing growing resistance. Juárez learned of rebellions erupting in a number of states and in June, 1855, he returned to Mexico to participate in the struggle for liberty.

He reached Acapulco by a most devious route and presented himself, to be used in any capacity, to General Juan Alvarez who was the principal leader of the maturing rebellion against the corrupt Santa Anna. Juárez did not identify himself, nor was he known by sight to Alvarez who was not impressed with this poorly clothed, unprepossessing dark-skinned Indian who was so anxious to serve. When it was discovered that the little Indian (he was only five feet in height) could write, he was assigned to write letters for the general's signature. It was only when a letter from Ocampo addressed "Al Sr. Lic. Don Benito Juárez" * arrived at the general's headquarters that he learned, with much embarrassment, the identity of the modest volunteer.

The government was rapidly disintegrating and Santa Anna, ever the opportunist, saw the handwriting on the wall and departed for a self-imposed exile, for the second time in his career.

Alvarez headed the new government and named Juárez as Minister of Justice and Public Instruction. In this capacity he drew up a law which inaugurated a new era of reform in Mexico. The *Ley Juárez* (the Juárez Law) seems modest enough by present day standards but at the time it aroused the bitter opposition of the Church, the professional army elite and the hacendados. The Ley Juárez set civil courts above those of the Church and the army. That principle was implicit in the American Constitution of 1787 and is standard practice in every country which has any pretensions to democracy. This law was followed shortly by the Lerdo Law which was aimed at destroying the economic power of the clergy by forcing them to sell Church lands. The essence of both laws was incorporated in the liberal, democratic constitution of 1857.

The laws had barely been promulgated when a storm of furious protest by the conservatives split the country. Their pronouncement accused the new leaders of being atheists, men without principles who profaned the churches and attacked priests and nuns and who "are preparing mourning, bloodshed, devastation and rapine for the Mexican Nation. . . . " Pope Pius IX joined the verbal fray " . . . to con-

---

* "Lic." is the title, abbreviated, for lawyer. "Don" is the title of distinction given to persons of stature.

demn, to reprove, and to declare null and void the said de-
crees and everything else that the civil authority has done in
scorn of ecclesiastical authority and of this Holy See. . . . "
It was an astonishing performance, in the middle of the
nineteenth century, to see the Pope still assuming worldly
powers in declaring the laws of a sovereign nation "null and
void." The fifteenth-century Church, holding fast to medieval doctrines, had not yet caught up with the nineteenth
century and its doctrines of liberalism.

Following the elections of 1857, Juárez was called on to
serve in the cabinet of the new president, Ignacio Comonfort. Dissension among the leaders plus an invasion of the
capital by the counter-revolutionary army sufficed to bring
about Comonfort's resignation, with Juárez succeeding to
the presidency. He may have been president, but he was a
president without a capital, without funds, without an organized army—a fugitive.

The fugitive President and his staff made their precarious
way to a small Pacific port in Colima. Then began an amazing odyssey. It was their intention to set up their government
in friendly Vera Cruz on the Gulf of Mexico. The President
and his aides sailed from Colima to Acapulco to Panama;
then went by rail across the isthmus to Colón; by ship to
Havana and from there to New Orleans; finally from New
Orleans to Vera Cruz where they were greeted by an enthusiastic, cheering crowd and a twenty-one gun salute.

The three years of the War of the Reform were filled with
all the horrors and atrocities attending civil war. Tens of
thousands were killed. There were murders, arson, betray-
als, disaffections, intrigues and counter-intrigues. Through
it all, the patient, imperturbable, black-frocked Indian lawyer held the reins of government firmly, guided changing
cabinets through a number of crises, and finally rode into

the capital in his black carriage to occupy the National Palace on January 1, 1861. Immediately he faced problems. The government was bankrupt, commerce almost at a standstill, customs receipts were pledged to pay off a mountain of foreign debts, agriculture—the economic blood of the Republic—was dying, and the conservatives continued to fight on in a dozen different areas. Help might have been forthcoming from Abraham Lincoln, who admired Juárez and who had every intention, after his election in November, 1860, to extend whatever aid was feasible. However, Lincoln had his own troubles starting even before his inauguration in March, 1861. The outbreak of the Civil War in the United States ended any hopes Juárez may have entertained of securing aid from that quarter.

The Mexican people, still reeling from the bloody civil war, had to suffer even more. Napoleon III of France, with dreams of an expanding empire to rival his more famous uncle, undertook to back Mexican reactionaries, who were willing to sell their country to a foreign power rather than live under Juárez. Appointed by Napoleon III as Emperor of Mexico, Archduke Maximilian of Austria took up residence there, innocently and falsely assuming that he had the support of the Mexican people. In actuality his reign was enforced by the presence of French troops to whom were allied the most conservative forces of Mexico—most of the regular army officers, the wealthy ranchers and merchants, and the Church. Now Juárez had the formidable task of leading his countrymen in war against one of the greatest powers in Europe as well as continuing the struggle against reaction in Mexico.

The War of Intervention dragged on for five interminable years, ending in 1867 with the complete defeat of the French and their reactionary Mexican allies. Maximilian, who had called Juárez and his supporters bandits and announced that they were to be executed, was himself executed on the orders of an unrelenting Juárez. In the museum at Chapultepec in Mexico City, there stand side by side the ornate, luxurious gilt carriage of Maximilian and the simple, unadorned black carriage of Juárez—mute reminders of two different ways of rule.

The Republic was at peace at long last. But there was no peace for Juárez. His personal life, which had been distorted with years of fighting, exile, involuntary separations from his family and the deaths of five of his twelve children, was given a new blow with the prolonged illness of his devoted wife, Margarita. When she died on January 2, 1871, he arranged for a secular funeral which shocked the orthodox Catholics. Still, the funeral procession was viewed by multitudes of silent, grieving people. To them the despondent Don

The execution of Archduke Maximilian and two of his Mexican generals by Mexican republicans. This was the ignoble end of Napoleon III's attempt to extend his empire to the Americas.

Benito showed his usual impassive countenance, but there was no question about his profound sorrow. Did he speculate whether his personal sacrifices were indeed worthwhile? If he had his life to live over, would he not have been the same man—devoted to family *and* to his compatriots? What had happened to his longing to return to his idyllic mountain village?

During his presidency, Juárez continued to live most simply. He dressed simply, wearing a white shirt, string tie and the plain black suit that had become his trademark, as had the simple black carriage used for both state and private occasions. In a country known for its palace plots and assassinations, it was all the more remarkable that the President always went about unescorted. While public officials were notorious for accumulating large sums of money, Juárez lived on his modest salary. He shunned display of any kind, and appeared indifferent to the popular homage consistently given to him. It might be charged that his sole vice was his concentrated addiction to his job.

The arts and letters took on new life during his regime. Secular schools were opened, challenging the monopoly of Church educational institutions. Mexico was blessed with an efficient and *honest* Minister of Treasury, Don Matías Romero, who had been a close associate of Don Benito for many years. Industry began to prosper, feebly, and Indian agricultural communities, aided by the government, began to improve slightly.

But there were complications which would throw Mexico off the road to continued peace and freedom. Rivalry developed among several political aspirants including two of the Indian's closest cooperators. One was Sebastián Lerdo de Tejada, author of the Lerdo Law. The other was General Porfirio Díaz, who had been Juárez's student at the Institute and who had gone on to become the most loyal and most efficient officer in the War of the Reform and the War of the Intervention. Lerdo and Díaz became presidential candidates to compete with the incumbent Juárez in the regularly scheduled election of 1871.

No one received a popular majority, and the election was thrown to Congress as stipulated by the election laws. Juárez

Porfirio Díaz and his principal advisers. Díaz was president and dictator of Mexico until the Mexican Revolution terminated his thirty-four-year regime.

was declared President, but Díaz cried foul. He issued a pronunciamento, then a Plan, and revolted. The uprising was quickly crushed, but he continued to prepare for a more propitious time.

Juárez suffered a severe heart attack and died on July 18, 1872. Lerdo then assumed the Presidency only to be driven out by Porfirio Díaz in 1876. The great dream of Juárez, the Man of Law, was quickly shattered and replaced by the rule of force. Díaz ruled Mexico from 1876 to 1910, thirty four years of police-state tyranny, with its own peculiar variety of "law and order."

Great men, like Juárez, are indispensable to progress. Although his achievements were not permanent, aborted by the Porfirio dictatorship, Juárez lives on as a source of inspiration in the continuing struggle for human dignity. Of all the famous men in the history of the Americas, no one was warmer, more humanistic, no man purer in spirit and action. For the leaders of La Causa, Juárez holds a special place of honor.

> Seek justice from tyrannical
> governments not with your hat in
> your hands but with a rifle
> in your fist.
> Zapata

Zapata    The *porfiriato,* the dictatorship of Porfirio Díaz, came to an end in 1910. For ten years thereafter Mexico was convulsed with revolution. One of the outstanding revolutionary leaders, hero to the Mexican-Americans today, was Emiliano Zapata.

As Juárez put himself in the service of the Nation, Zapata placed himself in the service of the *campesino* and the peón, the small farmer and the serf. Whereas Juárez rose above the confines of his native state and its problems, Zapata concentrated on the agricultural problems of the southland. This does not mean, however, that Zapata's stature as a genuine leader is any less, for like Juárez he is a continuing source of inspiration to Mexicans and Mexican-Americans.

The revolutionary leaders in 1910 had diverse aims: to create a democratic republic; to revise and update the liberal constitution of 1857; to expel, or at least to limit, foreign capital exploiting Mexico's natural resources and her people; to initiate labor reforms; to recover the personal, so-

Emiliano Zapata, agrarian chief and one of the
leaders of the Mexican Revolution.  He and
other Mexican patriots are continuing sources of
inspiration to Chicano leaders.

cial and property rights of the Indian (*Indianismo*); to undertake agricultural reforms. The Zapata movement, more than any other, imposed on all the actors on the political stage the problem of agrarian reform in Mexico. The Zapatistas sought to resolve the problems afflicting the small farmer—the *campesino*—and the peóns. And since the majority, in the area where Zapatismo operated, were Indians and mestizos, the agrarian question was inextricably related to the cause of the Indian.

Zapata was born in 1879 in the little village, or *pueblo,* of San Miguel Anencuilco in the southern state of Morelos (named for Father Morelos of independence fame). Emiliano had inherited from his father, a Zapotec Indian, a small plot of land. That placed him a rung higher on the social ladder than the majority of the Indians, who owned no land.

The small plot did not yield enough to subsist on. Zapata supplemented his living by sharecropping on neighboring plantations and by serving occasionally as a muleteer. Like his fellow campesinos he was illiterate; he was a small farmer, a simple, unsophisticated, hard working man of the people concerned with his own personal problems and the problems of his colleagues in the immediate neighborhood.

These problems escalated during the Díaz dictatorship. Big planters found that sugar cane production was profitable and their insatiable hunger for land led to angry confrontations with the Indian village proprietors of small plots and of *ejidos,* pueblo land used in common by the Indians. The *ejido* was a modernized version of the Aztec *calpulli,* likewise a communal form of agriculture. Díaz' policies encouraged the big hacendados who were forcing the Indians off their small individual-owned plots and who were wiping out the *ejidos.* Sharecropping and peonage were on the increase.

A basic Indian organization was the village council, usually made up of a few—four or five—elders who had long experience in fighting for land and water rights. In September of 1909, when Zapata was only thirty, he was elected by his peers to the presidency of the village council. The council elders believed in making way for younger men whom they felt were better suited to deal with the rapidly changing times. The most pressing immediate problem arose in connection with a new real estate law passed by the newly elected governor, a Díaz man. The villagers were determined to resist it, as well as any new oppression.

In the course of resisting the new law Zapata urged his fellow villagers to take up arms to defend their fields. They did not require much urging. Word of this action spread rapidly and Zapata became military *jefe,* chief, of his own village and two nearby pueblos, Moyotepec and Ayala. In this district, Zapata became recognized among the Indians as arbiter of all disputes about land titles, whether individual or *ejido,* whose existence was challenged by the new law.

Meanwhile Francisco Madero, a wealthy capitalist intellectual and reformer, had pronounced and issued his Plan. He was supported by General Pascual Orozco and General Pancho Villa in the north, plus other revolutionary conspirators, especially in Mexico City. Ten months of plotting, followed by Orozco and Villa fighting in the north and Zapata's armed campesinos taking charge in the south, were climaxed by Díaz' resigning and going into voluntary exile. Early in the uprising, Zapata threw his support to Madero because of his great promises about land reforms.

Once in office, Madero compromised and procrastinated, but Zapata would not yield an inch. The land belonged to the people, and the people would decide how it should be divided. *Tierra Libre Para Todos, Tierra Sin Capataces, Sin*

*Amos.* Free Land For All, Land Without Overseers, Without Bosses, was the slogan of the Zapatistas.

In his Plan of San Luis Potosí, Madero had proposed restitution of land. At a meeting with Zapata, Madero pointed out that the complications could not be ironed out easily, that legal procedures took time, and that Zapata should disarm his bands. While it was true that the big planters were taking advantage of the situation, he assured Zapata it would only be temporary, and that after land surveys, judicial proceedings, and so on, everyone would get his due.

Carbine in hand, Zapata strode over to the seated president and pointing to the latter's gold watch said, "Look, Señor Madero, if I take advantage of the fact that I'm armed and take away your watch and keep it, and after a while we meet, both of us armed the same, would you have a right to demand that I give it back?" Madero agreed, adding that he would also demand an indemnity. "Well," Zapata retorted, "that's exactly what has happened to us in Morelos, where a few planters have taken over by force the villagers' lands. My soldiers—the armed farmers and all the people in the villages—demand that I tell you, with full respect, that they want the restitution of their lands to be got underway right now."

By mid-1911 the Madero-Zapatista alliance was at an end, and warfare broke out. In November, the southern revolutionaries published their Plan of Ayala, in which they openly renounced their support of Madero, set up their own revolutionary junta, and devised a program of nationalization of land and redistribution of land to the poor farmers. So, the revolution was on again.

The Zapatistas grew in numbers and influence. At one time Zapata commanded an army of 40,000. That army was never defeated, and the agrarian movement spread throughout the south, covering much more than the state of Morelos where Zapatismo had originated. Land reform was initiated and carried out by armed campesinos who drove rich planters out. Zapata declared that "As long as there is a single armed campesino I will not permit that the haciendas hold on to the lands of the villages."

Zapata led his men against the federal government for eight years. During that time the federal government went through several changes of leaders. Madero was assassinated by one of his generals, Victoriano Huerta, whose dictatorial rule was opposed by a number of revolutionists including Zapata. Following the deposal of Huerta, General Venustiano Carranza became First Chief in 1916, and was elected President in 1917. The jockeying for power from 1913 on of rival generals like Villa, Obregón, Orozco, Calles, Rodríguez, in a maze of shifting alliances, saw former allies become enemies and vice versa. There was a loose unity among the dissidents who opposed Madero. For example, Villa and Zapata saw eye to eye, briefly, in their anti-Maderismo. All formed a temporary, informal agreement in fighting against Huerta. After Carranza was installed in office, Villa fought against him in the north, and the Zapatistas continued their guerrilla warfare in the south.

As far as Zapata and his followers were concerned, Revolution was meaningless unless it brought with it immediate resolution of the agrarian question. They would not accept any compromises, legal procedures, or constitutional guarantees that were not translated into simple seizure and division of the land by the campesinos themselves. The Constitution of 1917 which was modeled on the Juárez Constitution of 1857, included the now famous Article 27, a radical solution to the agrarian question. It wanted only implementation to satisfy Zapata and the campesinos and since that implementation was not immediately forthcoming, Zapata fought against the Carranza government.

Zapata led his men in incessant raids against haciendas, and against federal troops whose leaders were incapable of dealing with the Zapata tactics. Neither Zapata nor his men wore any distinctive uniform. They wore their everyday peasant clothing and bandoliers filled with bullets. Without the bandoliers, they were campesinos working in the fields—and hiding from the federals was no problem. It was the same for Zapata, who lived with his men, worked with them, ate with them, dressed like them. He was their jefe, known and respected, but he was foremost a campesino.

When federal troops deployed against the Zapatistas, tactics varied. Generally large-scale battles were avoided, especially when the southerners were outnumbered or when they confronted troops equipped with overwhelmingly superior armaments. The use of mass killing weapons like the awesome machine gun and the most modern artillery transported by rail had come into vogue. Such munitions were not manufactured in Mexico and had to be purchased, a situation which excluded everyone but large institutions, such as the federal government, which had either the money or the necessary credit. Zapata had neither.

Much of Zapata's weaponry came from the enemy—taken in battle, in raids, in the ambushing of trains. That was an unreliable source and while it proved sufficient to keep the federal troops occupied, there were never enough weapons to make possible a definitive victory for the Zapatistas. Their reliance on guerrilla warfare frustrated the federal commanders, who simply were unable to come to grips with the hundreds of Zapatista armed bands whose members were soldiers one minute and campesinos the next.

Zapata's men ranged throughout most of the south. The honesty and dedication of Zapata could not always be extended to all of his officers or to all the many individual bands who pledged allegiance to their general, but who were not subject to his immediate surveillance or control. Raids on haciendas, therefore, were not always military or economic in objective. There were instances of rape, sacking and arson, for the Indians exacted the most primitive means of revenge for the many centuries of oppression. Zapatismo-agrarianismo-Indianismo was not pure; large-scale revolutionary movements never are.

The Zapatista movement remained the principal obstacle to the establishment of peace in the republic. Failing to defeat Zapata, despite the superiority of federal troops and their equipment, a desperate President Carranza resorted to a crass, but effective maneuver which resolved his problem. He managed to bribe one of Zapata's officers, Jesús Guajardo. For $50,000 and promotion to brigadier-general Guajardo set a trap for his leader. Zapata, despite some suspicions, came out of the hills early in the morning of April 10, 1919, to discuss with his subordinate the transfer of a large amount of munitions which were in the latter's possession. Zapata and ten of his men walked through the gates of the hacienda, where they were to confer, walked between a guard of honor, a bugle sounded the honor call, and the guard of honor fired point-blank volleys at the General and his aides.

Guajardo exhibited the corpse to prove beyond any doubt that it was Zapata himself who had been thus assassinated. Carranza and his supporters were overjoyed. The "Attila of the South" was dead. And, they hoped, so was Zapatismo.

Many Indians refused to believe that their beloved leader was dead. They were sure that he would return any day, and until that time they would continue to fight. Much to the chargin of the federal government and of the hacendados in the south, the Zapatista movement continued. Bereft of its leader, the movement lost its organization, but the struggle for land persisted for many years.

Today Zapata is a national hero in Mexico. Monuments, memorials, street names and more commemorate the great agrarianist. Some of the most popular murals and paintings done by the world famous Diego Rivera and José Clemente Orozco, artists of the Revolution, are of Zapata and his followers, or deal with the Zapatista-campesino theme.

Among Mexican-Americans, Zapata is a favorite hero. Most particularly this holds true among the small farmers in the Southwest, whose primary concern is the resolution of the agrarian problem.

A mural by José Clemente Orozco showing the Zapatistas—the dedicated followers of General Emiliano Zapata.

Thinkers prepare the Revolution;
bandits carry it out.
Mariano Azuela

**Villa**   Pancho Villa was a picturesque, swashbuckling figure, somewhat in the tradition of the legendary Joaquín and other "Robin Hoods." For some Mexican-Americans, Villa is the more appealing, rather than Juárez or even Zapata.

The future general of the Revolution was born Doroteo Arango on June 5, 1878. When he was a young man he killed the son of his patrón for having raped his sister. He fled his birthplace, the village of Rio Grande, in the state of Durango in the north, and adopted the name of a legendary bandit, Francisco Villa. The nickname "Pancho," an affectionate diminutive for Francisco, remained with him for the rest of his life.

Until the Revolution broke out in 1910, Villa pursued the life of a bandit. Legend has it that he robbed the rich and gave to the poor. Undoubtedly much of the legend is true. It is also true that he and his cutthroats pillaged, rustled cattle, raped, whored, murdered, and shot up towns. Many of these exploits were senseless, without any political or even humanitarian motives.

When the revolution against Díaz commenced, Captain Villa and fifteen men joined in support of Madero. Their motive is not clear. Perhaps it was because Villa was afforded an opportunity to do legally what he had been outlawed for in the past.

He proved to be a capable and fearless leader who rose in rank to general. When Madero was assassinated in 1913, Villa and his army of the north campaigned against dictator Huerta. Villa received aid from the United States which opposed the Huerta regime. By this time he was no longer just

General Pancho Villa, revolutionary hero and
bandit chief.

a bandit, but had become dedicated to the cause of the Revolution, and to the cause of the campesino and the peón.

Once Huerta was overthrown, Villa continued as general in the north, at first supporting, then opposing President Carranza and his régime. So it was that Villa found common cause with Zapata, likewise fighting against the Carrancistas. He was the scourge of the north and became popular as the "Friend of the Poor," "The Centaur of the North," "The Hope of the Indian Republic."

In the spring of 1915, General Alvaro Obregón, a federal officer with considerable experience, moved north to confront General Villa and his Division of the North. Obregón had been studying the battles in France and had learned that French infantry were being senselessly slaughtered in mass attacks against carefully prepared German defense positions. He had his troops dig in near the town of Celaya, 135 miles northwest of Mexico City. They constructed zigzag trenches, heavily sandbagged and protected by barbed wire throughout the area. A number of machine gun nests were well placed to afford interlacing fire; artillery, commanded by a German Army officer, was strategically located; the cavalry was kept under cover and at the ready.

Villa, overconfident and inexperienced in the fine points of modern warfare, recklessly threw his men against the carefully prepared defense. After one day of fierce fighting, Villa's men were sent back in retreat. Obregón prudently refrained from pursuing his enemy. He spent the next week reorganizing and obtaining more supplies and ammunition, correctly calculating that Villa would attack again.

Villa had learned nothing from the first attack and threw his men—infantry and cavalry—into wave after wave of frontal assaults, only to be mowed down by shrapnel from the artillery and devastating machine gun fire. Villa's famous crack cavalry troops, the Dorados, were wiped out

An historic photograph of Generals Obregón,
Villa and Pershing taken when the two Mexican
revolutionary leaders received permission to
pass through United States territory. Obregón
and Villa subsequently fought against each
other, and Pershing led the punitive raid into
Mexican territory in pursuit of the elusive
Villa.

and finally the infantry panicked. Villa lost ten to twelve
thousand men, killed and captured. The Revolution was
broken, but he tried once more.

He managed to recruit another army and to obtain more
ammunition so that about two months later he felt ready to
attack the hated federals once again. And once again, near
León, Villa ordered his gallant men against well-entrenched
federal troops, who again decimated his army. Villa as a
revolutionary general was finished.

But Villa the bandit was not finished. With several hundred men, he continued to be the scourge of the north.
They raided mines, ambushed trains, pillaged haciendas and

towns. On March 9, 1916, Villa and a few hundred men crossed the border and invaded Columbus, New Mexico. Why? A show of pure bravado? A raid to obtain ammunition? A desperate gamble to provide a spark that would embroil the United States and Mexico in war? A vengeful attack upon the hated "barbarians of the North" who had officially recognized Villa's enemy, Carranza, as the head of the Mexican government? There is only speculation, no official explanation for Villa's raid upon the American town.

American troops in Columbus were caught by surprise by the 2:30 a.m. attack. They finally drove off the marauders, but not until after dozens of innocent men and women were robbed and killed.

The press in the United States enlarged upon the incident and screamed for revenge. So did the border inhabitants, and the army. President Wilson reluctantly ordered General John Joseph "Black Jack" Pershing to pursue and capture Villa. Pershing commanded three troops of cavalry, two infantry regiments and two batteries of artillery in the punitive expedition into Mexico.

Villa the bandit-guerrilla chieftain was more than a match for the West Point trained general. The Mexican was on familiar ground and had the support—sometimes voluntary, sometimes fear-inspired—of the people. Pershing pursued an elusive Villa for nine months, only on occasion coming into contact with the enemy. The objective of capturing or killing Villa remained unaccomplished and it was a frustrated Pershing who withdrew on the orders of President Wilson. The President had finally come to an agreement with Carranza who had protested the American intervention from the outset. Besides, the possibility of war with Germany was becoming more and more a probability. Pershing's failure to defeat Villa is a source of great elation for Mexicans and for many "anti-gringo" Mexican-Americans. There are

Villa's cavalry just prior to an attack upon Torreón, April, 1914.

reasonable grounds for resentment against the violation of Mexico's sovereignty.

Villa continued his raiding forays including two into Texas. But his star was on the wane. Villa and Villaism were on their way out.

After Carranza was assassinated in May of 1918, Villa retired. The Provisional President Adolfo de la Huerta (not to be confused with the General Venustiano) granted to the "Centaur of the North," the "Friend of the Poor," 25,000 acres, an hacienda, and a personal bodyguard of fifty of his

soldiers whose salaries were paid by the government. Villa was far from being a Juárez.

On July 20, 1923, after several unsuccessful attempts had been made, the retired hacendado was assassinated by eight men probably hired for the job by General, now President, Obregón. A year after the burial, vandals unearthed Villa's remains and hacked off his head, no one knows for what reason. Luís Valdez, a Chicano leader, the director of El Teatro Campesino of the farm workers of California, has written a play entitled *The Shrunken Head of Pancho Villa*. In it the shrunken head cries out to a headless Chicano boy, "There's the body and here's the head. Let's get together!"

Good-bye, my beloved land,
Now I am going away.
I go to the United States
Where I intend to work.

For I am not to blame,
If I abandon my land;
Poverty is to blame,
That holds us in misery.
From "An Emigrant's Farewell,"
a Mexican <u>corrido</u>

## CHAPTER VIII

# Twentieth-Century Strangers in Their Own Land

WHEN THE STATUE OF LIBERTY WITH ITS NOBLE INSCRIP-
tion was erected, the "golden door" to immigrants was already closing. Orientals were soon effectively excluded from
the United States, and after World War I a quota system
sharply limited the number of immigrants from Europe. No
restrictions, however, were placed on immigrants coming
from countries in the Western Hemisphere.

The first large wave of Mexican immigrants arrived during the period from 1910 to 1920. Some were fleeing the
devastating effects of the Revolution; some were encouraged
to enter to meet the relative labor shortage brought about by
America's participation in World War I. During the depression of the 1930's, immigration fell off sharply and, in fact,
many Mexicans returned to their homeland. The second
large wave began shortly after Pearl Harbor, in December,
1941, when once again the United States had a relative
labor shortage.

The great majority of Mexicans went to Texas, New Mexico, Arizona and California. Smaller numbers went to Colorado, Minnesota, Michigan, and a very few were found in other states from Oregon to New York.

The following table shows the ebb and flow of Mexican immigration from 1900 to 1968:

| | |
|---|---|
| 1900-1909 | 24,000 |
| 1910-1919 | 173,000 |
| 1920-1929 | 588,000 |
| 1930-1939 | 28,000 |
| 1940-1949 | 54,000 |
| 1950-1959 | 293,000 |
| 1960-1968 | 386,000 |

The numbers of *legal* immigrants represent only part of the total of Mexicans who crossed the border. Two other groupings have to be taken into account to fill out the picture: the illegal entrants, and those who were admitted for temporary work. During World War II, the demand for labor was so great that Mexicans were encouraged to enter the country on temporary work permits; some stayed a year or even longer. In 1942, there were 4,200 such temporaries, or *braceros* (those who work with their *brazos,* arms). The tempo increased rapidly thereafter; for the three-year period 1943-1945 an average of 50,000 braceros entered, and during the 1950's as many as 400,000 a year were welcomed by employers in the United States. After 1965 braceros were no longer permitted, supposedly.

Illegal migration has been a daily occurrence from 1848 to the present. The lack of adequate border patrols until 1924 made crossing easy; and the few patrols, when there were any, were easily avoided. Mexicans crossed for just a day's outing, or in pursuit of legitimate business of a temporary nature, or to visit friends and relatives, or even to settle permanently. That they were violating an international law probably never crossed their minds. On the American side, the inhabitants were not disturbed, for the numbers of Mexicans who came, prior to 1910, were few and they had been accustomed to the traffic much of which was not unwelcome. At the same time, Americans were crossing the border into Mexico in the same way and pretty much for the same reasons.

Effective border patrols were set up in 1924 and as the border thus became more formalized, illegal crossings were treated as such and deportations were not infrequent. When the authorities, and the American employers, wished to shut an eye to the illegalities, there were no problems. When, on the other hand, it suited them to carry out the letter and the spirit of the law, they arrested, prosecuted, punished and deported. Once the bracero program started, the number of illegal entrants increased, encouraged by employers. They contracted with labor smugglers, "coyotes," to bring unskilled workers across the border. An extremely lucrative business, it became highly organized. A "coyote" would receive ten to fifteen dollars from every recruit. The recruits would be turned over to a labor contractor who would sell the Mexican to the prospective employer for a fee of fifty cents to one dollar. In addition to that fee, the labor contractor charged the Mexicans for transportation expenses and food consumed *en route*.

The "coyotes" and the labor contractors cheated anyone and everyone. Sometimes the "coyote" would collect his ten dollars and disappear. Labor contractors would squeeze the Mexican for excessive transportation and food allowances. Carey McWilliams, the talented journalist, author, and editor, writes of a special type of agent, a man-snatcher, who would steal Mexican labor to sell the same crew to another employer, sometimes performing the operation several times in a few days. Such thefts were so common that labor contractors, McWilliams reports, resorted to locking up their crews at night under armed guard in barns, corrals, and warehouses.

Naturally there are no precise statistics about the number of illegal entrants. From the 1880's on, the number undoubtedly exceeded ten thousand annually. During World War II and thereafter, operation "wetback" developed. The opprobrious term "wetback" was applied to Mexicans illegally entering the country; the assumption was that such trespassers were swimming the Rio Grande. However most came by truck or afoot, and that meant that the authorities were in collusion with the "coyotes," labor contractors and the em-

Mexican laborers trying to cross the border at Calexico, California, February, 1954, in the hope of finding work in the fields of Imperial Valley. The big growers in California encouraged this mass movement to compete with domestic labor and to impede unionization.

ployers. When they wanted to do so, the authorities did, at times, crack down, and it is estimated that in the year 1953, 875,000 "wetbacks" were apprehended. Over 4,000,000 were deported between 1950 and 1960.

Not counting the "wetbacks" or those who are in the country on temporary work permits, the number of Mexican-Americans now in the United States is between five and a half and six million, over eighty percent of whom are in the Southwest. In 1969, they were distributed as follows:

| | |
|---|---|
| California | 2,200,000 |
| Texas | 1,630,000 |
| Arizona | 225,000 |
| Colorado | 180,000 |
| Total Southwestern U.S. | 4,500,000 |

President John F. Kennedy reminded us that, except for the Indians, we are all immigrants or descendants of immigrants. The overwhelming majority of all the immigrants to the United States started out as laborers, skilled and unskilled. That was true of the Mexicans who worked in the fields, orchards, vineyards, on the railroads, in mines, on the livestock ranges, in the canning and packing plants—to mention the principal occupational areas. Textbooks give much credit to the outstanding individuals who contributed to the building of this country. It is at least equally true that labor, the labor of immigrants, including the Mexican-Americans in the Southwest, contributed as much to help build America.

In the fields the Mexicans were relegated to the arduous task of "stoop" labor. It is called this from the position field hands must assume in picking cotton, melons, peas, potatoes, cucumbers, lettuce, tomatoes, beets and similar products of roots, vines and bushes. It is at harvest time, when the crops must be picked rapidly under the broiling sun with temperatures reaching 110 degrees, that stoop labor is mostly employed. Readers who have gardens or have ever worked on a farm will appreciate the extreme discomfort and fatigue that accompany stoop labor. One summer, when I was young and more foolish, I worked as a gardener—for two long weeks. I remember very vividly one hot day of a mere 92 degrees spent in pruning a large bed of geraniums. The boss demonstrated briefly how to pluck dead blossoms and extract weeds. Simple enough! At the end of twenty minutes, being a city youth quite unaccustomed to stoop labor, my back ached. After forty minutes, my back and legs were in agony. At the end of one hour I *pleaded* with my very kind boss to permit me to do some alternate labor. Field hands, including children under twelve years of age, had to perform stoop labor ten and twelve hours a day; and there were no "very kind" bosses to whom they could plead.

Mexicans helped build the Southern Pacific and the Santa Fe railroads. The rail lines of the Southwest and the West employed Mexicans in section crews and other semi-skilled and unskilled jobs. Often, as in the case of such railroads as the Santa Fe, Rock Island, Great Northern, and Southern Pacific, Mexicans made up the majority of the unskilled laborers employed on the lines.

In Texas, California, Oregon and Washington, Mexican-Americans have been employed in the canning and packing houses.

The growing sugar beet industry exerted an increasing demand for Mexican-American field labor. Sugar beet acreage is found principally in California, Michigan and Colorado; it spread to Ohio, Minnesota, Montana and North Dakota.

With few exceptions, immigrants have been relegated to

"Zoot-suiters" in a peaceful demonstration in Los Angeles, June, 1942, climaxing a period of turbulence during which Chicanos and Blacks were the principal victims of racial violence.

the most unskilled and menial tasks. The pattern continued with the Mexican immigrant, the newest to come to this country in large numbers. The economic pattern of discrimination is only one aspect of the hapless plight of the Mexican-American. The difference in language and sometimes of skin color make it easier for supremacists to perpetuate economic and social discrimination.

The Sleepy Lagoon Case and the
Zoot Suit Riots   It is in the *barrios,* the urban neighborhoods of the Mexican-Americans, that the prob-

lems exist in their greatest complexity. The majority, perhaps eighty percent, of Mexican-Americans live in urban areas, a trend that commenced early in this century and accelerated during the past thirty years.

Between 1930 and 1970 Mexican-Americans urbanized more rapidly than Anglos or non-whites. In a few cities, like Laredo and Brownsville, Texas, they form a majority of the population. They are a majority in several counties in Texas and New Mexico. In San Antonio, San Francisco and Los Angeles they constitute a large percentage of the total population. The Mexican-American population of Los Angeles is second in number only to the population in Mexico City.

Most of the barrios are overcrowded slums with poor sanitation, poor sewage, poor lighting, roach-infested substandard housing, filth, disease, juvenile delinquency, all the foul elements that characterize any slum of any American city.

In all the wars fought since the Spanish American War, Mexican-Americans have served with distinction in all branches of the armed forces. However, serving in the armed forces is no guarantee, minorities have learned bitterly, that life at home will improve. During World War II, when this country was committed to erasing Nazism and other varieties of fascism with their racist doctrines, Mexican-Americans at home were victims of covert and overt discrimination and much worse.

The racist attacks upon Mexican-Americans on the West Coast can be understood better when one sees them in relation to the peculiar atmosphere that emerged following the attack on Pearl Harbor by the Japanese on December 7, 1941.

Immediately after the attack about two thousand aliens suspected of Axis sympathies were rounded up, including

a few hundred Japanese subjects who were potential sabo-
teurs or spies. Some West Coast citizens were not satisfied.
They had been gripped by a panic kept alive by sensational
stories in the press and the racist speeches of some political
leaders and others who would profit by the elimination of the
Japanese farmers in the area. A campaign developed to remove all Japanese and Japanese-Americans (Nisei) from the
region. On February 19, 1942 the President authorized the
army to remove about 112,000 Japanese and Nisei from
Washington, Oregon, California and Arizona and to place
them in concentration camps politely called "relocation
camps." This unprecedented action has been assessed as the
greatest single violation of civil rights in American history.

With the Japanese removed, the sensation-mongering
press turned its attention to Mexican-Americans, who were
logical scapegoats, especially in California. A "crime wave"
in which Mexican-Americans were the selected targets hit
the front pages of the Los Angeles press. Muggings, vandal-
ism, robberies, burglaries, rapes and a few murders, (the
normal, sordid features of city life) were vividly and sensa-
tionally headlined. The number of crimes probably did increase during the war years. The Mexican-American was
accused arbitrarily of being the most responsible. Young
people, teenagers through the early twenties, were especially
suspect.

One aspect of the social life of many young Mexican-
Americans was the street gang or club, a social organization
typical of youngsters living in ghetto areas in every major
city of the country. Such clubs were often rivals, with disputes over "turf," or territory, and over girls; sometimes the
rivalry was intensive enough to end up in physical conflicts.
During the winter and spring of 1942 the press played up
incidents involving groups of Mexican-American youth and

also crimes actually committed by or attributed to this minority group. The time was ripe, after some eight months of build-up, to blow up a particular incident. This ugly incident, which took place in Los Angeles, is now known as "The Sleepy Lagoon Case."

On the night of August 1, 1942 two rival gangs, the "38th Street Gang" and the "Downey Boys" engaged in some scuffling. Early the following morning, near a deserted gravel pit filled with water that was used as a swimming pool by Mexican-American youth, the badly beaten body of a "Downey Boy" was found. He was rushed to the General Hospital where he died. There were no knife or gun wounds; the autopsy showed that he had died as a result of a fracture at the base of the skull.

The police arrested twenty-four young Mexican-Americans, allegedly members of the "38th Street Gang," and charged them with murder. The affair became known as the "Sleepy Lagoon Case" when an enterprising reporter gave that name to the "swimming pool," the site at which the victim had been found.

Seventeen of the young men were tried in a mass trial conducted in a semi-lynching atmosphere. It resulted in the conviction of nine on charges of second degree murder and assault, of three on the charge of first degree murder, and of five on lesser charges. A Sleepy Lagoon Defense Committee was organized and chaired by Carey McWilliams, lawyer, historian, journalist and onetime Chief of Division of Immigration and Housing, Department of Industrial Relations, State of California. McWilliams had long been active on behalf of Mexican-Americans and other minority groups in California.

While the Committee was raising funds and preparing an appeal, it was hounded by the press and by a witch-hunting state legislative committee, the Tenney committee, investigating communist and other subversive activities. Contributions to the Defense Committee came from G.I.'s from all over the world.

The trial of the seventeen might not have attained historical importance if there had not been some rather strange proceedings connected with it. Starting around the same time as the trial, a Grand Jury of Los Angeles County was called to investigate the growing "crime wave," and heard reports from several experts. The substance of one report, given by an "expert" who was an officer in the Sheriff's department, was that Mexican-Americans were given to crime, and that the youth were delinquent partly as a result of the slums in which they lived and partly because of the pervasive atmosphere of discrimination and segregation around them. But, the part of his report that gained the greatest publicity, and which was used to build up mass hysteria alleged that:

> The Caucasian, especially the Anglo-Saxon when engaged in fighting, particularly among youths, resort[s] to fisticuffs and may at times kick each other, which is considered unsportive: but this Mexican element considers all that to be a sign of weakness, and all he knows and feels is a desire to use a knife or some lethal weapon. In other words, his desire is to kill, or at least let blood. That is why it is difficult for the Anglo-Saxon to understand the psychology of the Indian or even the Latin, and it is just as difficult for the Indian or the Latin to understand the psychology of the Anglo-Saxons or those from Northern Europe. When there is added to *this inborn characteristic* that has come down through the ages, the use of liquor, then we certainly have crimes of violence. (Emphasis added.)

The "expert" Lieutenant E. Duran Ayres also stated that "crime is a matter of race" and that since the Mexican was part Aztec, and the Aztecs practiced human sacrifice, it was natural for him to have a "total disregard for human life . . . universal throughout the Americas among the Indian population. . . ."

Here was grist for the mill of the sensationalist press, for racists and for the police. McWilliams states that this part of the pseudo-scientific report was quoted by Radio Berlin, Radio Tokyo and Radio Madrid as proof that Americans supported the racist doctrines of Hitler. The report was enthusiastically endorsed by the sheriff, and the police now had "scientific" grounds for their attacks upon Mexican-Americans who were biologically impelled to criminal behavior!

The Grand Jury committee did not agree with the racist report. It had heard reports from many other experts which more accurately placed the responsibility for the many problems on segregation and on discriminatory practices in public places, in jobs, housing, and education. It made a number of recommendations designed to ameliorate the explosive situation, but they were generally ignored by the public and by the several agencies which were in a position to carry out changes for the better. Only a few feeble attempts were initiated, and these were generally drowned in the hysteria that had been successfully created by reactionary elements in the state.

A drive on "Mexican" youth got under way. On the nights of August 10 and 11, six hundred were rounded up; one hundred and seventy-five were arrested on charges of possession of such weapons as knives, chains and guns. On October 30, seventy-two "Mexicans" were arrested. Intermittently, young men and women were harassed and insulted, and there were continuous charges of police brutality.

In such a hate-filled atmosphere other incidents were inevitable. Some of the worst were the so-called Zoot Suit Riots.

Mexican-American youth had taken to wearing apparel

which marked them off from most other American young people. The zoot suit was a long suit coat coming to well below the knees, with trousers which were pleated at the waist, rather wide at the thighs and narrowing down at the ankles with pegged cuffs; to this ensemble was added a long, low-hanging watch chain. Hair style was an important feature also; long and heavily greased, it contrasted with the more popular "crew-cut." Mexican-American girls also affected a different dress style: short skirts, net stockings, and high-heeled shoes.

Distinctive dress worn by youth as a status symbol has been common for many decades before and since World War II. Ethnic minorities who dress differently are easily singled out for adverse criticism which does not limit itself to aesthetic evaluations. If a "crime wave" is being emphasized by the mass media, ethnic minorities come in for more than their share of verbal and even physical attacks. It has been estimated that about five per cent of Mexican-American youth in California were delinquents. However all zoot suit wearers were presumed to be criminal types.

Instances of delinquency, such as beatings administered to some sailors (often by men, not youths) were used to mount up an hysterical campaign against all zoot suiters, and "Mexicans" and Blacks. The riot that took place in June of 1943 in Los Angeles subsequently spread to other cities in California and elsewhere in the country.

After about two months of planning, two hundred sailors armed with clubs, chains, stones and the like invaded the barrios. Other servicemen and civilians soon joined them. Theaters were invaded and "Mexicans" ordered out; street cars were stopped; restaurants, bars and other public places were raided. Zoot suits were ripped off, young men and women were beaten, some severely enough to require hospitalization.

Not only zoot suiters were attacked; anyone suspected of being "Mexican" was victimized by the raging mobs. A black defense worker had one eye gouged out. A Mexican-American mother protesting the arrest of her fourteen-year-old daughter was cracked across the jaw with a nightstick. Clashes between Mexican-American youth, some of whom began to organize defense groups, and servicemen and vigilantes increased daily. The riot lasted a full week.

The police generally did not interfere. Either they looked the other way, or often looked on, and gave aid to the servicemen. Editorials appeared in some newspapers justifying the attacks of the mobs. One might imagine a Texan version of a Greek chorus chanting "Remember the Alamo!"

A typical "shack-town" of cotton pickers near Fresno, California. The prevalence of such miserable conditions of migratory workers, affecting Chicanos mainly, motivated Chávez to organize a union of farm workers.

After the riots came investigations. A Grand Jury investigated; it acknowledged the failure of the community to follow up the recommendations made by the Grand Jury committee the previous year. Communist party leaders charged that much of the trouble was being stirred up in the barrios by the *sinarquistas,* members of a Mexico-based fascist, pro-Nazi party. Thereupon the Tenney Committee investigated the communist leaders, not the sinarquistas whom other investigators had proved were in league with the Nazis. Governor Earl Warren also initiated an investigation which concluded that the zoot suit problem was not a racial one. Yet all the victims had dark skins: Mexicans, Mexican-Americans and Blacks.

Meanwhile the Sleepy Lagoon Case was still awaiting a hearing on appeal. It reached the District Court of Appeals in 1944. A unanimous verdict reversed the lower court's decision and was highly critical of the conduct of the trial judge and of the prosecuting attorney. Then the entire case was dismissed for lack of evidence. However, the seventeen youngsters had already spent two years in jail because the lower court had refused to grant bail. And during those two years the alleged "crime wave," the mysterious death of one "Downey Boy," the wearing of zoot suits, had been used to effect a senseless, hysterical attack upon Mexican-Americans throughout California. There is some validity to the suggestion that the Good Neighbor Policy, designed to cement friendly relations with the Latin American countries, should start in the American Southwest.

Racial clashes affecting Mexican-Americans diminished after the zoot suit riots in the summer of 1942, not to disappear completely. Isolated incidents were daily occurrences in every city of the Southwest where there were large numbers of Mexican-Americans. Since none of these incidents approached the large-scale character of the week-long riot in Los Angeles, they did not cause undue alarm nor did they merit national publicity. The issues were there all the same, and growing.

During the next two decades, characterized as being "quiet" by Manuel P. Servín, Associate Professor of History at the University of Southern California, there were no riots, no big clashes between Mexican-Americans and other groups. However all the problems of the braceros, and the problems of growing urbanization, poor education, poor housing, job discrimination—all of which could trace their antecedents to the period immediately following the American conquest of the Southwest—were accelerating, festering.

The situation came to another dramatic climax, with La Huelga in 1965.

In May, 1972, Chávez, the charismatic leader
of the United Farm Workers, AFL-CIO,
announced a second national boycott of a
farm product.

To be a man is
to suffer for others.
César Chávez

## CHAPTER IX

# Campesinos of the Southwest

BEFORE THE SPECTACULAR SUCCESS OF CÉSAR CHÁVEZ IN California, there had been other attempts to organize the farm workers in the Southwest.

The first farm workers organization in California was the Fruit Workers Union, organized in 1903. Between 1912 and 1917 the I.W.W., Industrial Workers of the World, or the Wobblies, had minor, brief successes. From 1928, when the Imperial Valley exploded in a strike of farm workers, there were sporadic strikes, none successful. In the 1930's the Communists were the most active in the field of organizing this neglected branch of labor.

The depression which began at the end of 1929 hit agriculture particularly hard. Prices of farm products tumbled, and so did wages. In the "good" year of 1929 average daily wages, without board, were $3.56. If a farm worker had twelve months employment, which was impossible, he might earn $900 a year. By 1933, the average daily earnings had been depressed to $1.91. To subsist, barely, everyone in the family had to work in the fields, even children of ten, and younger! At one hearing of the state labor board in California in 1933, testimony was given by Roy Domínguez, seven years of age, that he picked 65 pounds of cotton in the farms of San Joaquín valley from 7 a.m. to nightfall. He was paid at the rate of 60¢ per hundredweight, which meant that he was paid 3¢ an hour.

Many of the farm workers of the Southwest were migratory, traveling from harvest to harvest, from county to county, from state to state. They had no permanent residence. This meant little or no education for the children, loss of the right to vote, none of the simplest comforts of life in the country that boasted of the highest standard of living in the world. For homes, the migratory families lived in work camps provided by the owners of the "factories in the fields." The following description of such camps was given, in 1934, by a commission appointed by the National Labor Board:

> We inspected the camps of the pea-pickers, and know that they are similar to the camps that will serve as places of abode for workers in the field when melons are gathered. This report must state that we found filth, squalor, and entire absence of sanitation, and a crowding of human beings into totally inadequate tents or crude structures built of boards, weeds, and anything that was found at hand to give a pitiful semblance of a home at its worst. Words cannot describe some of the conditions we saw. During the warm weather when the temperature rises considerably above 100 degrees, the flies and insects become a pest, the children are fretful, the attitude of some of the parents can be imagined and innumerable inconveniences add to the general discomfort.

A little over thirty years later, Secretary of Labor Willard Wirtz, after visiting the worker camps in California, said, "I'm glad I hadn't eaten first. I would have vomited." The progress of thirty years!

Some of the first strikes of farm labor, during the depression of the thirties, began in the Imperial Valley of California. They were called by the Mexican Mutual Aid Association, but without any success. The Association was not equipped for such a task for it was not a union but, as implied in its name, a mutual aid society. The American Federation of Labor had never given any attention to the plight of the "unskilled" farm workers. The gap was filled by the Cannery and Agricultural Workers Industrial Union, a creation of the Communist Party. In 1933 and 1934, under its leadership, thousands of Mexican, Filipino and other farm workers participated in dozens of ineffectual strikes throughout California and in other states. The growers employed legal and illegal means to defeat the union. Vigilantes were used. Organizers were beaten and jailed; Mexican-Americans were harassed and even deported; lawyers employed by the union, by the American Civil Liberties Union and other interested groups were driven out of town, arrested and jailed on charges of vagrancy. Members of the clergy sympathetic to the farm workers were intimidated. The growers unleashed a veritable reign of terror.

In February, 1935, the Communist party ordered the dissolution of the union in order, said the leaders, to concentrate on working within the ranks of the mainstream of labor and to eliminate all the dual unions which they had organized in opposition to the A.F. of L. Between 1937 and 1939, the C.I.O. tried to organize the farm workers but gave up the difficult fight for easier pickings. The agricultural workers were left without any effective labor organization for almost thirty years.

After World War II, farm labor did not share in the gains being made by organized labor throughout most of the country. The Magna Carta of labor, the Wagner Act of 1935, legalized the right of collective bargaining for workers but it specifically excluded farm workers. Subsequent amendments, like those incorporated in the Taft-Hartley Act of 1947 and the Landrum-Griffin Act of 1959, did not remedy the defect so that farm workers do not enjoy the same legislative protection afforded most workers.

The squalor and poverty of the 1930's still prevailed. In the 1960's: infant mortality was 125% higher than the national rate; maternal mortality was 125% higher than the national rate; influenza was 200% higher than the national rate; accidents were 300% higher than the national rate. The life expectancy for a migarnt worker was 45 years, at a time when other Americans could expect to live for 70 years. Children working in agriculture are excluded from child labor and school attendance laws. Farm workers are discriminated against in the social security laws. Without labor contracts, there is no job security, no overtime pay, no holidays and vacations with pay, no sanitary toilets and drinking water, no health insurance, no rest periods, no grievance procedure, and so forth.

The AFL-CIO, which did much to advance the interests of workers in existing unions, ignored the farm workers, the majority of whom in the Southwest were and are Mexican-Americans. It was a Mexican-American, a farm worker for most of his life, who picked up the challenge— César Estrada Chávez.

Chávez was born in 1926 on the tiny farm his father owned near Yuma, Arizona. During the depression the farm was lost and the family joined the migrant workers. Starting at age ten Chávez worked, when he could, with the rest of the family in the fields. Given little opportunity for education, he managed to attend about thirty different schools in the course of the family's constant wandering, and finally had to drop out in the eighth grade. The family came to rest

A portion of the picket line in front of La Casita Farms, Texas in June, 1967. Note the Aztec-like eagle in the banner.

in San Jose, California, continuing to work as farm hands in the neighboring fields.

Chávez remembers vividly instances of discrimination against his people. NO DOGS, NO MEXICANS were commonly displayed. WHITE ONLY was meant to exclude not only Blacks, Indians and Orientals, but also Mexicans and Mexican-Americans who, ironically enough, are tabulated as white, or Caucasoid, by official census takers. Once, when Chávez was seventeen, he refused to sit in the segregated section of the movie house in Delano and was thrown out into the street.

From his father, the young Chávez learned the importance of union organization. In 1939 the elder Chávez had joined and was active in the C.I.O. farm union. There were several strikes in which the Chávez family participated, without one victory. From a Catholic priest, Father Donald McConnell, César learned much about labor history and through the priest he met Fred Ross, an organizer for the Community Service Organization (CSO).

Chávez quit the fields to become a community organizer for the CSO. He stayed with the CSO for ten years during which time he gained invaluable experience, dealing with such diverse problems as health laws, welfare problems, registering new voters, rent strikes, taxes, discrimination against minority groups. He resigned his national directorship to work with the farm workers of California.

It was slow, plodding, financially unrewarding but spiritually satisfying work. Without any aid, initially, from the powerful AFL-CIO, Chávez patiently brought farm workers into the National Farm Workers Association (NFWA).

The first important meeting of the NFWA took place in Fresno in September of 1962. The platform was decorated with a flag designed by Manuel Chávez, César's cousin. It was a huge red flag with a black Aztec eagle in a white circle. Some mistook the symbolism for Communism, some for Nazism. Manuel won the day when he cried out, "When that damn eagle flies, the problems of the farm workers will be solved." The flag was adopted as the emblem of the union.

Chávez seized upon the opportunity presented when Public Law 78 (P.L. 78) lapsed at the end of 1964. This law had made it possible for the growers to bring in large numbers of braceros at harvest time. They and the "wetbacks" coming into the country for temporary periods earned much more, however small by U.S. standards, than they would have gained in Mexico. The growers wanted P.L. 78 to stand because, they argued, Americans would not take the difficult jobs of stoop labor. What they meant was that they were able to get cheap labor and to use the braceros and "wetbacks" against the union organization. The temporary status of the legal and illegal workers acted as an effective block to union organization; and their presence enabled the growers to maintain depressed wages for the permanent resident. The end of the bracero program made it easier for the farm workers union to function. So it was that in 1965 Chávez called the first strike in Delano, California. The strike lasted five long years, culminating in victory for the union men. It is a saga of human sacrifice, frustration, tragedy and triumph that deserves its own history.

The strike started in the vineyards at Delano and soon spread throughout the state. The first major victory and breakthrough took place in 1966 when the fields owned by Schenley, one of the large American liquor corporations, settled with the union, and shortly thereafter most of the vineyards that produced grapes for the wine industry also signed up. From that point on the strike affected only the growers of table grapes. The Schenley victory was notable not only in that wages were raised from the average of $1.40 per hour to a minimum of $1.75, but more importantly in that a union hiring hall was established. The union hiring hall guarantees that the union may exercise the necessary controls for equitable hiring practices for the permanent resident farm workers and to prevent the hiring of illegal "wetbacks."

The table grape growers fought on for another four years. The tactics they used ran the gamut of every anti-labor de-

In 1966, Chávez led grape strike pickets and sympathizers in a 300-mile, 25-day march from Delano, California, culminating in this mass demonstration at the steps of the Capitol in Sacramento.

vice known. Pickets were threatened and beaten. Provocateurs and labor spies were employed. Shotguns were used to destroy picket signs and to blast car windows. Guns were fired over the heads of pickets. Cars were run off the road. Speeding trucks flew down the road brushing the picket

lines; several workers were hit, one was run over and permanently crippled. (This worker, Manuel Rivera, is now employed on a farm that settled with the union.) Picket lines were sprayed with pesticide. The hired guards of the growers made no nice distinction between men and women. Women pickets, who were on the lines every day, suffered the same fate as their men folk—threatened, beaten and jailed. Arrests and jailings were almost daily occurrences; 44 pickets, who had been warned against using the word "Huelga!"

and had defiantly persisted in so doing in order to attract the Mexican strikebreakers, were jailed. To offset the shouts of the pickets, the growers had radios blaring away in the fields, brought up cars and trucks near the picket lines and counter-shouted with bull horns and loudspeakers, and had car horns and bells adding to a wild cacaphony of noise.

The growers had the support of state and local officials from Governor Ronald Reagan on down to town and county leaders. The union and its leaders were even stigmatized with the Communist label. Those who did so used as proof the fact that the strike was supported by the Communist party, (as it was by all the New Left, and by liberals, and by humanitarians, and by labor leaders, and by Senator Robert Kennedy, and by Senator Williams of New Jersey, and by religious leaders, and by high school and college youth, in short by individuals of every political persuasion). Still, the logic of the Tenney Committee and other such witch-hunters is that any movement or organization that earns the support of any radical organization must be itself radical.

Chávez was constantly under personal attack, and received a number of death threats. He was a Communist, an atheist. He was a Labor Czar, living sumptuously on the backs of the unsuspecting, poor farm workers. (Chávez, like all the other union leaders, received $5 a week as strike pay.) He was an outside agitator who, according to *Barron's,* a prestigious national business and financial weekly, "never soiled his hands with such toil himself." In Delano, the authorities offered evidence that Chávez had a very poor academic and attendance record in the Delano schools. (Chávez had never attended any school in Delano.)

The AFL-CIO and individual unions belatedly began to give financial support to the strikers; and, at long last the union was recognized and affiliated to the AFL-CIO with the new name United Farm Workers Organizing Committee (UFWOC). To help meet the very modest $40,000 a month strike fund, contributions came from individuals from all over the country. All the money thus raised was never enough to cover ordinary union expenses—telephone, leaflets, picket signs, rent, strike pay of $5 per week, *et cetera.*

One can measure the "radicalism" of the union by observing the gains won: higher wages; overtime pay; vacations and holidays with pay; rest periods; elimination of speed-up tactics (whereby one very fast pacesetter paid by the employer compels everyone to maintain an inhuman speed); grievance and arbitration procedures; gloves and masks to protect the farm workers spraying pesticides and other chemicals. (Between 1950 and 1961, according to Truman Moore's *The Slaves We Rent,* "3,040 farm workers were poisoned in California by pesticides and other farm chemicals. Twenty-two workers and sixty-three children died.") There would also be toilets in the field. This last "radical" change remedies a very elementary situation for the farm workers and it should be a source of considerable relief to the consumers of farm products: health authorities have noted that poliomyelitis, hepatitis and other serious diseases are transmitted by human feces in the fields. Last, but not least important, the workers won union recognition and the right of collective bargaining.

The success of the strike was made possible by Chávez' energetic use of the national boycott of grapes initiated in New York in January, 1968. In April of 1969 the striking grape workers issued a proclamation in which they declared that:

Grapes must remain an unenjoyed luxury for all as long as the barest needs and basic human rights are still luxuries for farm workers. The grapes grow sweet and heavy on the vines, but they will have to wait while we reach out first for our freedom. The time is ripe for our liberation.

High school and college young men and women helped picket stores that violated the boycott. The boycott spotlighted, for the whole nation, the miserable conditions of the grape workers in particular and the farm workers in general. Nationally prominent figures, like Senator Robert Kennedy, gave their support to the grape pickers. The public was impressed with the charisma of Chávez and his doctrine of non-violence. It was the first successful national boycott in the history of American labor.

Chicanos marched four hundred hot miles from the Rio Grande valley to the state capitol in Austin to highlight their demands for higher wages—and a better life in general.

Violence, however, did attend the incredibly long strike. It was a traditional feature of the growers' tactics, and many union members responded in kind. While Chávez himself was quite militant, he deplored any violence. Since he was the leader of the union, however, he felt responsible for any violations of his creed of non-violence. As an act of penitence he began a fast early in February, 1968. The Franciscan priest, Mark Day, offered mass every night during the fast which lasted until March 11. Senator Robert Kennedy flew to Delano to be at the side of Chávez on the last day of the fast and to participate in a Mass of Thanksgiving attended by 8,000 people. A prayer in Hebrew, a Protestant sermon and Catholic ritual were combined to emphasize the unity of all creeds so important to Chávez. In his speech to the gathering, he said, " . . . the truest act of courage, the strongest act of manliness, is to sacrifice ourselves for others in a totally nonviolent struggle for justice. To be a man is to suffer for others. God help us to be men!"

Chávez, very much influenced by his reading of Thoreau, the first great American to practice civil disobedience, and of Gandhi, who carried it out so successfully a century later in India, presented a picture of machismo quite different from that associated with Pancho Villa or Joaquín.

Although the main concentration of the union was in California, it was active elsewhere—New Jersey, New York and Texas.

The organizer Eugene Nelson, who had had experience in the grape pickers' strike, was sent to Texas in 1966. The immediate task was to try to organize the farm workers in Rio Grande City, where La Casita Farms operated a highly efficient, modern fruit and vegetable farm of some 1,600 acres. The principal demand of the workers was that wages be raised from the current 40–80¢ per hour to the federal minimum standard of $1.25. The reader may judge for himself the reasonableness of this demand. At $1.25 per hour, or $10.00 for an eight-hour day, or $2,600 a year—on the assumption that work is available on a fifty week basis—the breadwinner of an average sized family of four would be only about $5,000 *behind* what is conservatively considered to be the minimum health budget requirements!

To dramatize the needs of the farm workers in La Casita Farms and of all the poor in Texas, a people's march was planned to the state capital, Austin. It began on July 10 and was to end on Labor Day. Forty-three people, led by Father Antonio Gonzales, wearing a cowboy hat and a Star of David, and the Baptist Reverend James L. Navarro set out from San Juan, 387 miles from Austin.

It was not until late August, after the marchers had patiently plodded many miles through the blistering summer heat, that Texans became aware of the seriousness and significance of the march. More and more individual community leaders—priests, rabbis and ministers, politicians, and officials of the state AFL-CIO—spoke on behalf of the farm workers and expressed their horror at the unspeakably miserable conditions of the poor in the land of oil millionaires and cattle barons.

The rapid growth of sympathy for the farm workers was met by the growers with the usual verbal barrage that the union organizers and their supporters were "outside agitators" and "Communists," and with piteous cries that meeting the demands of the farm union would force the growers out of the Rio Grande valley. The number of marchers increased to hundreds, the shout of "Viva La Huelga!" grew ever louder, and support increased.

On August 30 Governor Connally and two other state officials drove fifty miles from Austin to New Braunfels to

The national boycott of grapes initiated by
Chávez gained support throughout the nation.
In May, 1969, Times Square, New York City,
was the scene of one demonstration by
sympathizers. Many conducted picket lines,
distributed handbills and contributed money
to the striking grape pickers.

meet with the marchers. Connally and Father Gonzales em-
braced. But Connally went on to say that he had no intention of meeting with the marchers at the state capitol on
Labor Day or any other time.

Liberal politicians were presented with a golden opportunity on which they made haste to capitalize. If Connally
would not see which way the political wind was blowing,
other politicians long opposed to him hastened to Austin;
Senator Robert Kennedy, however, sent a telegram expressing his regrets. Dignitaries addressed the huge crowd and
many promises were made. No action. The farm workers
returned to their homes, resolved that their only recourse
was La Huelga.

Months went by. The union prepared. In May of 1967 a

record-breaking melon crop was anticipated; the growers and the union leaders knew that the highly perishable melons had to be picked within four to six weeks. Gilbert Padilla, vice president of the NFWA, issued an ultimatum to the growers that they negotiate or the crop would rot on the ground. The growers replied by hiring Mexican "green carders" from across the border to offset the projected strike. "Green carders" were Mexicans who were issued temporary work permits on green cards. This was the growers' answer to resolve the crisis.

The union was determined to prevent the green carders from crossing the border in the first place, or failing in that maneuver, to prevent them from crossing their picket lines around La Casita Farms.

The Texas Rangers were assigned to keep law and order. That was not an unusual commission, but the Rangers were not accustomed to handling a strike situation. Keeping the peace and seeing to it that Texas laws were obeyed resulted in indirect support to the growers and led, almost inevitably, to clashes between the Rangers and the strikers. Picketers were arrested; some were beaten. The melons were picked by the green carders, who then returned to Mexico. The special task force of Rangers left the valley. The strike in Texas was lost, while it continued in California.

State and national investigating committees criticized the Rangers for appearing on the side of the employers, for improper dealings with the press (cameras had been seized and film exposed, and reporters had been harassed), and for violating the civil rights of the strikers.

After the victory of the grape pickers in California, many consumers blamed the increase in price for farm products on the rising wages of farm workers. However, the wages paid farm workers are only a very small part of food costs.

For example: in 1965, the year that La Huelga began, the retail price of one head of lettuce was 21¢ but the field labor cost was only 1.2¢ per head. The balance of the price is made up of other costs, including the profits of the grower, the shipper, the middleman and the retailer. In the instance cited, if the wages were *doubled* to 2.4¢ per head and *if* that additional cost were passed along from grower to the ultimate consumer, the increase in price would be only 1.2¢ per head. If the retail price should jump more than 1.2¢ then the responsibility rests on shoulders other than those of the field hands.

After five years of bitter strike, the success of the workers led by Chávez must be considered as minimal. Other than in California, few farm workers have been organized. The migrant workers remain the worst housed, the worst paid and the most exploited labor force in the nation. Illegal aliens, many of them from Mexico entering the United States to become migratory workers in the Southwest, pose an ever-deepening crisis. Many have a status no better than that of indentured laborers, and some are virtually slaves. Their competition with domestic labor enables employers to pay substandard wages and retards improvements in working conditions. In an article in *The New York Times,* October 3, 1971, Donald Janson charged that many farm labor offices favor the growers by disregarding federal regulations. Many local offices are staffed with former growers or friends or relatives of the growers so that while the federally funded state-operated offices are supposed to provide services for workers as well as growers, only the latter benefit. Laws on child labor, wages, hiring practices, and working conditions are openly violated by the big growers, who are becoming increasingly contemptuous of federal laws aimed at aiding the farm workers.

In Arizona, the Republican-controlled legislature passed

a controversial farm labor bill, signed by Republican Governor Jack Williams in May, 1972, and destined to go into effect in August, 1972. It aroused bitter protest by Chávez who gained the support of Senator George McGovern. The presidential aspirant said: "The action of the Governor of Arizona reflects a brazen indifference to the legitimate rights and needs of farm workers to organize and bargain collectively."

No fundamental change seems likely to take place in the immediate future that will ameliorate the miserable conditions of the migrant workers in general and the migrant agricultural workers in particular. One may only anticipate continuing struggles.

Like all the Chicano leaders, Chávez is proud of his heritage as a Mexican-American. He disagrees with those who boast, vaingloriously, of La Raza—the Race. Chicanos speak proudly of being part of La Raza, an all-inclusive term which may mean, variously: the Spanish-speaking people of the Western Hemisphere; the cosmic race of the mixture of white Europeans and the New World Indians; or that mixture plus the African Blacks; or the Mexicans and Mexican-Americans; or the oppressed Mexican-Americans seeking human dignity; or simply "soul," the Mexican-American version of the Black movement.

Chávez implies that the concept, not the term itself, is racist and is quick to point out that the union, now national in scope and affiliated with the AFL-CIO, includes Mexicans, Filipinos, Blacks, whites, Japanese and Chinese. "Our belief is to help everyone, not just one race. Humanity is our belief."

Chávez, then, is no mystic, no radical, no racist. He is a humanist above all. Politically he may be classified as a liberal, one who supported Robert Kennedy as presidential aspirant in 1968. A firm believer in non-violence, he supported and was supported by the Reverend Martin Luther King, Jr. Like King and other practitioners of non-violence, Chávez is militant and fearless. He has been jailed and threatened with death; he has organized and participated in marches to the California state capital and to the national capital; he has faced gun-toting sheriffs, militia and vigilantes. The terrorism of the growers held no terrors for this mild mannered, yet *muy macho,* much beloved leader of his people.

Since 1968 he has blossomed into being something more than a leader of farm workers. He spoke out forcefully against the use of poisons, pesticides and other chemicals in the fields. He supported the national strike for peace-in-Vietnam and convinced the members of his union that there was more to struggle for than the elementary demands raised in La Huelga. La Huelga was not only inextricably bound with La Causa, but La Causa had merged with what may be the new American Revolution.

Reies López Tijerina and his wife, Rose.
Tijerina is the Chicano leader who originally
focused on the land grants issue in New Mexico
before expanding the struggle to include
various political and social, as well as
economic rights of Mexican-Americans.

My land is lost,
and stolen,
My culture has been raped...
Rodolfo Gonzales

## CHAPTER X

# Whither Mexican-Americans?

WHILE THE ATTENTION OF THE NATION WAS FOCUSED ON the dramatic farm workers' strike and the grape boycott, other issues were being brought to the fore by Chicano leaders in the 1960's. One of these leaders, Reies López Tijerina, was active in New Mexico highlighting problems connected with the old Spanish and Mexican land grants.

Reies López Tijerina appeared suddenly in New Mexico as a hero of Mexican-Americans. What brought him into the national spotlight was the dramatic raid on the courthouse of the village of Tierra Amarilla in northern New Mexico on June 7, 1967.

Tijerina was born in 1926, one of ten children of a sharecropper, in Fall City, Texas. He alleges that he is descended from a colonial Spaniard who married an Indian princess of the Tejas (Texas) tribe. He also contends that a great grandfather was a large landholder who was murdered by Anglos and robbed of his ranch.

Beginning around 1960 Tijerina concentrated his energies around the issue of the old Spanish and Mexican land grants. His demands that the old land grants be reconstituted seem to be utopian. One might just as well demand the land be returned to the Indians from whom it was stolen in the first place.

As founder and president of the Alianza Federal de los Pueblos Libres (Federal Alliance of the Free City-States, which developed out of the earlier Alianza Federal de Mercedes) Tijerina reopened for public examination the land grants issue. In Tierra Amarilla the villagers responded warmly to his flamboyant speeches, reminding them that the 594,500 acres had been granted one José Martínez in 1832 by the Mexican Government. Originally much of the acreage was allotted for communal use by poor peasants, (a practice originating in Spanish law and custom and continued by the Mexican Government), while the property rights were retained by the Martínez family.

By 1910 the lands of the Tierra Amarilla grant had been lost to the original owners and were owned by individual Anglo-American ranchers and land speculators. The villagers claim that despite the transfer of ownership, the legality of which they also question, they still had the communal rights that were part of the original grant. Subsequently much of the land—only 10,000 acres are held by Mexican-Americans—had been bought by the National Forest Service (part of a federal conservation program that had begun as early as 1892 and continued in the 1950's) resulting in great profits to the land speculators, and deprivation to the small farmers. With justification the National Forest Service and its supporters stand for preservation and ecological controls. With equal justification the villagers protest that they have been building up, not destroying, the land and that the federal government prevents them from living on ejidos, as they had done for more than a hundred and forty years.

While it is true that these poor farmers, and big ranchers as well, have some grazing rights on the federal land, they must now pay for these rights, so that they cannot afford to graze all of their animals. Furthermore, they allege, lumber companies are getting rich on the lumber which they may take from the National Forest, while the poor people are limited to a few sticks for firewood. Therefore the economic conditions have worsened for the poor Mexican-Americans whose annual incomes are usually less than $1,000. If, they claim, their old ways of living cooperatively could be restored their condition would be immeasurably improved.

The militancy of the Hispanos, as the Mexican-Americans of New Mexico call themselves, mounted. In the spring of 1967, after having waited almost a year, a group of sheepherders who had expected to meet with an Assistant Secretary of Agriculture to discuss their grievances met instead with a regional forester. That official made short shrift of their complaints, not even bothering to wait for a number of latecomers who had intended to sit in on the meeting for which they had waited a year.

Shortly thereafter a mysterious outbreak of forest fires alarmed the authorities. At the same time Tijerina arranged a meeting of the Alianza to plan setting up roadblocks of the area claimed by the villagers. The night before the scheduled meeting, the state District Attorney had eighteen members of the Alianza arrested and jailed without charges. It was not until they were arraigned in the courthouse of Tierra Amarilla, that they learned that they were being charged with unlawful assembly.

On June 7, Alianza members—possibly with Tijerina present—stormed the guardhouse. They released the prisoners, shot up the building and one guard, and escaped with two hostages. To aid the local police, the National Guard was called out, complete with rifles, bayonets, tanks and helicopters. There was a mass roundup of Alianza members, and men, women and children were thrown into a corral and kept there overnight.

A trial was held a year and a half later at which Tijerina was charged with 150 crimes. After a most dramatic trial in which he acted as his own attorney, Tijerina was acquitted of all charges. However there were two old charges pending, and at a second trial he was found guilty on both counts. On January 5, 1970 he was sentenced to serve concurrent terms of one to five years and two to ten years.

While he was out on bail, Tijerina threw himself into the civil rights struggle in New Mexico. He challenged the educational system which denied to Hispanos much of their heritage, including the right to express themselves in Spanish. He is one of many Mexican-Americans who have forced the educational authorities to reexamine their educational standards and to give some consideration to the possibility of bilingual education. He was one of the organizers of the famous Poor People's March to Washington, D. C. leading, along with others, the Chicanos of the Southwest.

In Denver, Colorado, another Chicano leader, Rodolfo "Corky" Gonzales, directed his efforts to the political stage, emphasizing the present and future role of young Mexican-Americans.

Reading the early history of Gonzales one is reminded of Jack London's short story "The Mexican" in which a young Mexican-American, desirous of aiding the Revolution in Mexico, becomes a professional boxer to earn money to donate to the cause. Gonzales was a prize fighter as a young man, having chosen that career as a way out of poverty. He had earned an enviable reputation as a boxer, winning 65 out of 75 professional bouts, when he abruptly quit boxing in order to dedicate himself to La Causa.

Still, he had to earn a living, and being a man of many talents he drifted from one vocation to another. He has been a farm worker, insurance agent, government official, playwright and poet. He entered politics in Denver where he had unusual success in bringing out the ethnic vote in the 1960 presidential election. President Kennedy showed his appreciation by sending a personally autographed, framed photograph of himself and Gonzales in a friendly pose. He was also awarded five different positions: member of the Steering Committee of the Anti-Poverty Program for the Southwest, member of the National Board of Jobs for Progress, member of the Board of the Job Opportunity Center, President of the National Citizens Committee for Community Relations, and Chairman of the Board of Denver's War on Poverty.

Gonzales was soon frustrated by what he considered to be the "politics as usual" Democratic Party. In 1965 he founded *La Cruzada Para La Justicia* (The Crusade for Justice) attempting to galvanize Mexican-Americans into action, and especially into independent political action.

Chávez had his Plan of Delano, modeled on Zapata's Plan of Ayala; Gonzales has his Plan of Aztlán (an ancient place name of the Aztecs). It is a plan for the "nation" of Mexican-Americans which draws upon Aztec traditions. Whereas Chávez had emphasized the plight of the farm worker and has branched out in concern with problems of other Mexican-Americans, Gonzales from the beginning has directed his efforts to the needs of the barrios.

His poem *I am Joaquín* abounds with references to Joaquín, Pancho Villa and Zapata. A portion of it reads:

> I am Joaquín.
> I rode with Pancho Villa
>        crude and warm.
> I am Emiliano Zapata.

In Washington, D. C., during the Poor People's March, he declaimed:

> I am Joaquín
> in a country that has wiped out
> all my history,
> stifled all my pride.

and made specific references to the Indian and Mexican heritage of the Mexican-Americans. He loses no opportunity to talk about the history of his people.

He may be characterized as a revolutionary nationalist, dedicated to La Raza, who sees the awakening Mexican-American as "an emerging nation, a new breed."

In 1969 Gonzales organized a national conference of barrio youth, held in the Center of the Crusade for Justice in Denver. Fifteen hundred Chicano youths came from all over the country to participate in workshops in a wide range of fields from self-defense to philosophy and to listen to speeches glorifying La Raza. The Chicanos vowed to dedicate themselves to the "Spiritual Plan of Aztlán." Gonzales declared that the "call of our blood is our power, our responsibility, and our inevitable destiny . . . we declare the Independence of our Mestizo Nation. We are a bronze people with a bronze culture . . . we are a nation, we are a union of free pueblos, we are Atzlán."

Chávez has accepted the cooperation of Gonzales, but it is very doubtful whether he concurs with the extreme nationalism expressed in the latter's political philosophy. The area of agreement is sufficient, however, to effect a very loose, informal alliance around the burning issues of the farm workers and of the citizens in the barrios.

The widespread discrimination against Mexican-Americans

has been bitterly protested. The most glaring examples of social discrimination are in education and in housing, the two often going hand in hand. Segregated housing leads easily to segregated education. Segregated education cannot be equal, declared the Supreme Court in its famous decision in 1954. While the immediate reference, at the time, was to the segregation of Blacks, the majority Court opinion obviously holds true for the segregation of any minority.

In the larger cities of the Southwest, segregated schools have all but disappeared. The segregated school, where it exists, is not the worst of the evils befalling the education of

Rodolfo "Corky" Gonzales, Chicano leader in Colorado, demonstrates his support of José A. Gutiérrez, elected in 1972 as chairman of the executive committee of the Raza Unida party.

Mexican-American children. One is the language problem, and another involves culture differences. Spanish is spoken in the majority of the homes of Mexican-Americans. In school, the children have been warned against using, and sometimes punished for using Spanish in class or even on the school playgrounds.

Children with language handicaps have been given "objective" IQ tests and wound up in classes for the mentally retarded. A "tracking" system works to the disadvantage of Mexican-American children who receive inferior education from inferior teachers. Spanish is even derided by some teachers as an inferior language. The language of Cervantes, whose *Don Quixote* is acclaimed as one of the world's masterpieces of fiction; of José Echegaray, Jacinto Benavente y Martínez, and Juan Ramón Jiménez who were awarded Nobel prizes in literature; of Miguel de Unamuno, the great Basque philosopher; of Federico García Lorca, world famous Spanish poet and playwright; of the many renowned poets and novelists from Spain and from nineteen countries of South and Central America—the works of these illustrious men guarantee Spanish literature a place of honor along with the most famous in any language.

U.S. Representative Edward R. Roybal of California recently offered a brief explanation why fifty per cent of the young drop out of school before high school and another thirty per cent do not graduate. "Many of these kids don't speak much English but they are not permitted to speak Spanish in class. They don't learn anything and it makes them ashamed of their language. There aren't enough properly trained teachers to motivate them and the kids fall behind. They never catch up and pretty soon they get discouraged and quit." Whether they quit or graduate, they enter a fiercely competitive economic world where a caste system walls off the better-paying jobs and where minorities face a "last-hired, first-fired" job pattern.

Leaders of the Chicano movement in the Southwest, supported by some Anglo educators, are demanding bilingual classes, that the Spanish language be taught starting with elementary grades, and that, at the very least, children should not be discouraged from speaking their parents' tongue, in or out of class.

Recognizing the validity of the demand for bilingual education, Congress enacted special legislation, the Bilingual Education Act, which became law in January, 1968. Its implementation has been more breached than honored. To make the law effective in the Southwest (and in Florida, New York and wherever there are large numbers of Spanish-speaking people) would require the restructuring of the educational system, the special training of old and new teachers, the rewriting of textbooks. Teachers would have to know both languages and learn Mexican-American culture and history. The monetary cost would mount up to hundreds of millions of dollars. The money could be made available, but it is a question of priorities with defense, space programs and the like receiving the topmost spots. As of this moment, the Bilingual Education Act is not much more than another piece of paper containing noble words yet to be translated into action.

In December of 1971 the United States Commission on Civil Rights declared that minority group students in five Southwestern states were receiving an inferior education. In February, 1972, a report concludes that "the schools (in the Southwest) use a variety of exclusionary practices which deny the Chicano student the use of his language, a pride in his heritage, and the support of his community." The report goes on to criticize schools for failure to establish bilingual education programs and states that fewer than ten per cent of the schools in the Southwest offer courses in Mexican-American history, and that in some cases the textbooks evidence "an inexcusable Anglo-American bias."

In addition to suffering from the evils associated with poverty, Mexican-American children are burdened with humiliation and derision in school. Their customs are ridiculed. Their heritage is denied or falsified. School curricula do not include contributions of Mexicans and Mexican-Americans. There is no question of learning about Daniel Boone, Lewis, Clark, and Kit Carson. Chicanos charge that little or nothing is told about Cabeza de Vaca, Estevanico, Oñate, de Vargas, Kino, Serra, Portolá *et al.*

In the Southwest, where so large a percentage of the population is Mexican-American, the leaders of La Causa are demanding that the history textbooks be rewritten to conform more with the facts and thereby to give to their children, and to all others, a truer picture of the history of this country. It may be legitimately argued that throughout the country the schools should abandon the parochial attitude which gives short shrift to a significant portion of American history, that part of the heritage that is distinctively Spanish-Mexican-Indian. The time is long past that we should have to "Remember the Alamo." It would be far better to forget the Alamo and to learn Articles VIII and IX of the Treaty of Guadalupe Hidalgo.

To the degree that the formal school system is failing Mexican-American children, La Causa leaders are attempting to fill the gap. In the barrios of the Southwest, courses are being given in the Spanish language, Mexican-American culture and history.

The growing awakening of the Mexican-American has been manifested in recent years in the political arena. Using as a criterion the number elected to offices at various levels, the movement has not been strikingly successful.

In the national government, there is only one Mexican-American senator and his election is not a reflection of growing political power but of the continuation of the special state of affairs in New Mexico (See Chapter VI). Dennis Chavez was senator in the 1930's and 1940's; Joseph M. Montoya holds that office now. There are four Mexican-Americans in the House of Representatives: Edward R. Roybal, California; Henry B. Gonzales and Elijio de la Garza, Texas; and Manuel Luján, Jr., New Mexico.

Ezequiel Cabeza de Vaca, in 1916, was the first Mexican-American governor of New Mexico, or of any state. Octaviano Larrazola, born in Mexico and raised and educated

Joseph M. Montoya, Democratic Senator from New Mexico.

in New Mexico, was the second in 1918. David M. Cargo has been Governor since 1967. New Mexico has the largest number of Mexican-Americans in its state legislature—33. California, which has the largest number of Mexican-Americans, 2,200,000, has only one in its state legislature. Texas, with the second largest number of Mexican-Americans, 1,630,000 has 10 in its legislature. Colorado—1; Arizona —4. There is no Mexican-American serving as mayor in any of the large cities.

Elective office holding does not tell the whole story of the growing political participation of Mexican-Americans. Candidates for office are being presented where there never had been any before. There is growing activity in election campaigns at all levels, as indicated by increased voter registration, meetings, parades and speeches by leaders like Chávez. Both major parties make special appeals to win the "ethnic vote." Some contests at the local level are quite sharp, especially for posts on school boards, and for county and barrio appointive positions. In August, 1971, President Nixon appointed Henry M. Ramírez, a former migrant worker in California, as chairman of the Cabinet Committee On Opportunities for Spanish-Speaking Peoples. The expectation is that there will continue to be heightened political activity in the immediate future.

There are more than twenty-five barrio newspapers published in eighteen different towns and cities in California, Arizona, New Mexico, Texas, Illinois, Wisconsin, and Florida. These papers report local events, provide an avenue for protests and airing of grievances, and express diverse political views of the Chicanos. They also publish poems and short stories which are the literary expression of the traditions, the feelings and the aspirations of Mexican-Americans.

In the past year or so, since the end of the grape pickers

strike, there have been no major incidents that warranted sustained national concern. In Los Angeles there was a "minor" riot in September of 1970. The occasion was a protest rally and demonstration against the war in Indochina. Two persons were killed, 60 injured, 200 arrested and property damage was estimated at one million dollars. The reporter for *The New York Times* commented that the mood in the barrio, following the riot, was one of "alienation, hostility and tension. . . . Every sign indicates that this mood is spreading—here and throughout the Southwest—from the young to the not so young; from the poor to the middle class; from the dropout to the Ph.D.'s." He went on to point out that there were three major points of focus: police relations, political power and education.

In March, 1971 there was a peaceful Chicano march in San Juan, Texas. It was led by the Mexican American Youth Organization (MAYO) which has been compared to the Southern Christian Leadership Conference, the civil rights organization created by the late Martin Luther King, Jr.

In May of the same year there was a quiet, but militant protest by Chicanos in Texas voicing their displeasure over the appointment of an Irish-Canadian as bishop. Father Ralph Ruiz, national chairman of PADRES, organization of Mexican-American priests said, "One out of every four Catholics in the United States is Mexican American." (The Father is in error, or incorrectly quoted. A more accurate estimate would be one of eight or nine). "Yet we have only one bishop in the whole country. Why? You begin to wonder if the church is being fair or even loving." In a reply to Ruiz, Archbishop Furey said, "It is not wise of them to talk like this. Of course the church loves them. They just have to wait."

Wait? The Blacks heard that advice starting in 1865 and

have decided that waiting does not produce results. The Mexican-Americans are coming to the same conclusion.

The gap between the Church leaders and the priests working with the people in the barrios is but a continuation of what prevailed throughout the history of the Church in the New World. Some Mexican-Americans, including Chávez, recognize the dichotomy; their complaint is that the Church ought to minister to the poor as well as to the upper class. Others are not so tolerant, and argue that the Church has conspired with those in power, for it is itself a part of the power structure; nevertheless they respect the parish priest who does actively support La Causa.

On the surface, if we judge by the scarcity of front page headlines in the national press, there are no serious disturbances; there are occasional mild ripples, but no waves; there are isolated local incidents, but no major national upheavals; there are many leaders, but no accepted national leadership of the Chicanos. For the average American, there does not seem to be any cause for alarm. All seems to be relatively quiet.

However abundant evidence suggests that there is a sub-surface seething, a growing militancy among Mexican-Americans. The stirrings of this awakening minority, along with those of other minorities, notably the Black American and Puerto Rican, contain the explosive elements of what may be a new American Revolution.

# GLOSSARY

*barrio*—city district, usually a ghetto, in which most of the residents are Spanish-speaking.

*bracero*—hired, unskilled farm worker

*calpulli*—ancient Aztec farm cooperative

*campesino*—small farmer

*caudillo*—military or political leader; strong man

*corrido*—Mexican-style ballad

*criollo*—Creole, of Spanish descent born in the New World

*ejido*—cooperative farm community

*gringo*—derogatory term for whites

*grito*—cry of protest

*hacendado*—owner of hacienda

*hacienda*—large landed estate

*hidalgo*—originally, lowest rank of nobleman

*hispano*—term once used to refer to New Mexican resident who was of Mexican descent.

*huelga*—strike

*machismo*—term to denote manliness, virility

*mestizo*—offspring of white and Indian

*mulato*—(mulatto), offspring of white and Negro

*patrón*—master, landlord

*peón*—day laborer, usually tied to the land

*pronunciamento*—formal announcement of an uprising

*ranchero*—owner of a ranch

*rico*—term originally applied to rich Mexican-American in New Mexico

*vaquero*—cowhand; herdsman

*zambo*—offspring of Indian and Negro

# RECOMMENDED READINGS

ALIANZA FEDERAL   *The Spanish Land Grant Question Examined*

BECK, WARREN A.   *New Mexico: A History of Four Centuries*

BISHOP, MORRIS   *The Odyssey of Cabeza de Vaca*

BOLTON, HERBERT E.   *The Spanish Borderlands*
                   *Coronado*

CABEZA DE VACA, FABIOLA   *We Fed Them Cactus*

CALLCOTT, W. H.   *Santa Anna: The Story of an Enigma Who Once Was Mexico*

CARUSO, J. A.   *The Liberators of Mexico*

CASTANEDA, CARLOS E.   *The Mexican Side of the Texas Revolution*

CHAPMAN, CHARLES E.   *The Founding of Spanish California, 1687–1783*

FAULK, ODIE B.   *Land of Many Frontiers: A History of the American Southwest*

GALARZA, ERNESTO   *Strangers in Our Fields*
                 *Merchants of Labor: The Mexican Bracero Story*

GAMIO, MANUEL    *The Mexican Immigrant: His Life Story*
                 *Mexican Immigration to the United States*

GIBSON, CHARLES    *Spain in America*

GONZALEZ, NANCIE L.    *The Spanish Americans of New Mexico: A Heritage of Pride*

HAMILL, HUGH M., JR.    *The Hidalgo Revolt*

HARING, CLARENCE E.    *The Spanish Empire in America*

HORGAN, PAUL    *Great River: The Rio Grande in North American History*
               *Conquistadors in North America*

INTER-AGENCY COMMITTEE ON MEXICAN-AMERICAN AFFAIRS    *The Mexican American: A New Focus on Opportunity*

JONES, OAKAH K.    *Pueblo Warriors and Spanish Conquest*

MADSEN, WILLIAM    *The Mexican Americans of South Texas*

MATTHIESSEN, PETER    *Sal Si Puedes: César Chávez and the New American Revolution*

McWILLIAMS, CAREY    *North From Mexico*
                    *Factories in the Fields*
                    *Ill Fares the Land: Migrants and Migratory Labor in the U.S.*

MOQUIN, WAYNE AND VAN DOREN, CHARLES, EDS.    *A Documentary History of the Mexican Americans*

NABOKOV, PETER    *Tijerina and the Courthouse Raid*

NATIONAL ADVISORY COMMISSION ON FARM LABOR    *Farm Labor Organizing: 1905–1967*

NELSON, EUGENE    *Huelga: The First Hundred Days of the Great Delano Grape Strike*

OFFICE OF EDUCATION, WASHINGTON, D.C.    *The Mexican American: Quest for Equality*

PICÓN-SALAS, MARIANO    *A Cultural History of Spanish America*

PINCHON, EDGCUMB   *Zapata, The Unconquerable*
*Viva Villa! A Recovery of the Real Pancho Villa*

PITT, LEONARD   *The Decline of the Californios*

PRAGO, ALBERT   *The Revolutions in Spanish America: The Independence Movements of 1808–1825*

PRESCOTT, WILLIAM H.   *The Conquest of Mexico*

REED, JOHN   *Insurgent Mexico*

ROEDER, RALPH   *Juárez and His Mexico*

SAMORA, JULIAN, ED.   *La Raza: Forgotten Americans*

SIMPSON, LESLIE   *Many Mexicos*

SINGLETARY, OTIS A.   *The Mexican War*

STEINER, STAN   *La Raza: The Mexican Americans*

TANNENBAUM, FRANK   *Mexico: The Struggle for Peace and Bread*
*Peace by Revolution: Mexico After 1910*

TAYLOR, PAUL S.   *Mexican Labor in the United States: Imperial Valley*
*Mexican Labor in the United States: South Texas*

TIMMONS, W. H.   *Morelos of Mexico*

URENA, PEDRO HENRIQUEZ   *A Concise History of Latin American Culture*

VAILLANT, G. C.   *Aztecs of Mexico*

WEINBERG, ALBERT K.   *Manifest Destiny: A Study in Nationalist Expansion*

WELLMAN, PAUL I.   *Glory, God and Gold*

WOMACK, J., JR.   *Zapata and the Mexican Revolution*

## *FICTION*

CRICHTON, KYLE  *The Proud People*

FERGUSON, HARVEY  *The Conquest of Don Pedro*
  *Followers of the Sun*

FLORES, ANGEL, ED.  *The Literature of Spanish America* (4 vols.)

GARNER, CLAUDE  *Wetback*

EL GRITO  *El Espeso*

PEREZ, LUIS  *El Coyote the Rebel*

SIMMEN, EDWARD, ED.  *The Chicano*

VASQUEZ, RICHARD  *Chicano*

VILLARREAL, JOSE ANTONIO  *Poncho*

# INDEX

## A

Acton, Lord, 106
AFL-CIO, and farm
  workers, 176, 178, 182–
  183, 186, 190
Agrarian problems, in
  Mexico, 142, 145. *See
  also* Farm workers; Land
  ownership
Agriculture, in New Spain,
  22–23. *See also* Agrarian
  problems; Farm workers
Agustín I (Emperor of
  Mexico), 74–75
Alamán, Lucas, 73
Alamo, the, 97, 99, 100,
  202
Alarcón, Hernando de, 49
Alianza Federal de los
  Pueblos Libres, 194–
  196
Alvarez, Juan, 132–133

Alzate y Ramírez, José
  Antonio, 29
American Federation of
  Labor, and farm
  workers, 175. *See also*
  AFL-CIO
"Americans," origins of
  term, 65. *See also*
  Anglo-Americans;
  Anglo-Texans
Anglo-Americans:
  attitudes toward
  Californios, 78–79;
  heritage of, 4–5; in
  Mexican Southwest, 90–
  104; and settlement of
  Arizona, 121–122; and
  settlement of New
  Mexico, 116–120; and
  settlement of Texas, 91–
  93. *See also* Anglo-
  Texans
Anglo-Texans: attitudes